Traditional Soteriology:

Traditional soteriology is defined as the soteriological beliefs of the earliest church fathers (Ignatius, Justin Martyr, Irenaeus, Tertullian...) who held that:

- Man's nature is depraved and he is helpless to save himself.
- God, in His mercy, offers salvation to mankind through the substitutionary death of Jesus Christ.
- The atonement of the cross is not limited to a select group of individuals but is equally effective and offered to all who will believe.
- Upon hearing the call of the gospel, man stands accountable for his acceptance or rejection of the gracious call to repentance.
- Salvation is all of God, graciously given to those who humbly believe.

Salvation Through the Eyes of a Prodigal

A Defense of Traditional Soteriology from the Parable of the Prodigal Son

Dennis J. Harry Jr.

Pastoral Pen Publishing

Copyright © 2018 Dennis J Harry Jr.
Pastoral Pen Publishing (www.pastoralpenpublishing.com)
All rights reserved.
ISBN: 978-1732657304

Pastor Dennis J Harry Jr.
Needhams Grove Baptist Church
359 Needhams Grove Road
Robbins, NC 27325
www.needhamsgrovechurch.com

All rights reserved. No part of this publication may be reproduced, stored in a retrieval system, or transmitted, in any form or by any means, electronic, mechanical, photocopying, recording, or otherwise, with prior written permission of the author.

All Scriptural quotations are from the King James Version of the Bible.

**This book is dedicated to my
dad, Dennis J Harry Sr.**

I will be forever thankful for the influence and direction he placed on my life. He instilled in me a dedication to God's Word and a willingness to take up the cross of ministry and serve God faithfully.

Special Thanks

I want to thank my wife for her patience and understanding. Writing a book while being a husband, father, pastor, and student often left me writing late into the evenings on the living room couch. Thank you, Lorrie, for supporting me in all my ministry endeavors!

I want to thank Needhams Grove Baptist Church for their hunger for God's Word. Your desire to know the Scriptures drives me deeper in my studies!

About the Author

Dennis is no stranger to local church ministry. Growing up in a missionary's home, he has been in and around ministry all his life. Dennis received his undergraduate degree from Pensacola Christian College and will soon graduate from Piedmont International University with his Masters of Divinity. He has pastored for 14 years and is dedicated to preaching God's Word in a way that is accurate and true to what God has revealed through the Scriptures. He pastors Needhams Grove Baptist Church in Seagrove, NC, regularly writes articles for online and print distribution, and is the host of Let's Talk Church — a podcast for pastors and ministry leaders.

Let's Talk Church strives to be "a real discussion, about real church issues, with real church leaders." This is more than just a catchy phrase — it accurately describes the week to week discussion that Dennis has with local church pastors and missionaries. Discussion always centers around practical helps that will encouragement anyone connected to local church ministry. Episodes can be found at www.letstalk.church or on any of the major podcast directories.

Dennis also published Christian Worldview Parenting in the summer of 2018. Visit his website for more details!

www.djharry.org   www.letstalk.church   www.pastoralpenpublishing.com

Do you want to connect? Feel free to look up Dennis on social media. Facebook, Twitter, and LinkedIn (@PastorDJHarry) and Instagram Pastor.DJHarry

My Dad's Testimony

On July 6th, 1975 something took place that changed my life forever. You would assume it happened to me, but actually the circumstances of the this day had nothing to do with me...though they had everything to do with me.

My dad, Dennis Jackson Harry Sr., was raised in the Church of Christ and remembers clearly being baptized at an early age. He was told that his baptism along with good works would get him into heaven! With that wonderful news came years of doubt and fear. Deep down in his heart he knew nothing had changed — he had no confidence. He attended college, got married, and received a commission into the United States Navy. He proudly served for ten years and had all intention of making the Navy his career. His leadership, personality, and work ethic kept the promotions coming and life looked promising for this young married sailor.

Traveling overseas, visiting tropical ports...Navy life was a fun life! Though my parents were 'good moral people' and had been raised with a connection to church, the exciting Navy atmosphere was full of temptation and allure.   Drinking, smoking, dancing, parties, night life: my parents felt right at home in this environment and were having the time of their lives. As a side note, as my dad and I have talked through the years, it always bothered him that the one person tasked with being a spiritual influence (the chaplain), would sit at the bar and drink just like everyone else. Sadly, his presence confirmed over and again that they were just fine spiritually — if the chaplain was with them in the bar then they must not be all that bad.

Eventually, a family of two became a family of three. (I am the second of three children; my older sister [Lisa] is three years older than me and my younger sister [Sarah] is six years younger.) Lisa's birth didn't bring about much change. For the most part, my mom and dad kept up their normal social life. In the midst of their growing family, though, there was no avoiding the fact that my parents had nagging doubts about their eternal future. When I was born, however, something in my parents did change. The responsiblity of two children began to weigh on their minds. There was a nagging reality that life was no longer about them and they had a responsibility to bring up their kids in a moral home. The solution was simple — we need to take our kids to church. Having been raised in a church setting, my parents knew that it was the right thing to do. Without really thinking, the decided to visit local churches and so they naturally looked up the church that was closest to their house.

On July 6th my parents walked into Grace Baptist Church of Goose Creek, SC. Pastor Gerald Townsend greeted them before the service, and after the normal announcements and songs, he stood behind the pulpit and began to preach from Luke 15. He walked the congregation through the Parable of the Prodigal Son and began to preach on the lost eternal state of sinful man. Even as the sermon began, my dad stood firm on his profession of faith — he knew that he had been baptized and was trying to live a good life. As the sermon progressed, however, Pastor Townsend came to a pivotal point in the story. Luke 15:15-16 describes in vivid detail a scene that was eye opening for my father. The prodigal son is at the lowest of lows, helpless and hopeless, with no one to help and no way to save himself. It was at this moment that Pastor Townsend made a very simple point —sinful man is in the pig pen spiritually and no amount of good works can get him out.

The Holy Spirit conviction on my father was immediate. It was at that point that he realized that his best efforts were helpless to save — he was still in the depths of his sin and headed to eternity in hell. Right there at his seat he prayed a simple prayer. "Lord, I quit trying on my own and I trust in you!" At that very moment something miraculous happened to my dad. He was redeemed by the blood of Jesus, was adopted into the family of God, was restored to fellowship with the Father, and was given all the rights and privileges of a child of God!

My dad's life was changed forever through the Parable of the Prodigal Son!

Contents

Foreward 1
1 Salvation: The Defining Issue 5
2 Why Parables? 19
3 Scriptural Context 37
4 Cultural Context 44
5 Family Shame - Luke 15:11-12 55
6 Riotous Living - Luke 15:13-14 71
7 Feeding the Swine - Luke 15:15-16 84
9 I Will Arise - Luke 15:17-18 93
9 Repentance and Faith - Luke 15:18-20 107
10 The Father Ran - Luke 15:20 120
11 Sonship Restored - Luke 15:22-24 134
12 The Elder Son - Luke 15:25-30 157
13 Mercy Extended - Luke 15:31-32 170
Epilogue: Common Misconceptions 188
Recommended Resources 201
Connect With The Author 202

Forward

Why the Parable of the Prodigal Son?

    His posterboard message was simple...John 3:16. Though few people know his name, Rollen Stewart singlehandedly took one Bible verse and put it center stage at major sporting venues and important cultural events. During the 70's and 80's he took his simple message to the 1977 NBA Finals, the 1979 MLB All-Star Game, the Indianpolis 500, at least one Super Bowl, as well as appearing at The Masters golf tournament in Augusta, GA. It is reported that he also appeared at the royal wedding of Princess Diana! Stewart's message was not lost on the crowds, and he quickly became a popular attraction whenever he appeared

    Undoubtedly, John 3:16 stands as the most popular verse throughout recorded history. The Parable of the Prodigal Son isn't far behind; as parables go, it often tops the list of favorites among believers! A son that rebels. A father that loves unconditionally. A brother jealous of the celebration. This parable draws us into a torn relationship between a father and son and then exposes the cultural norms that should have finished off that relationship for ever! Instead, we see a son's humble repentance and a father's unconditional love! Sadly, we also see a scorned brother with no desire to rejoice. This parable is full of twists and turns. What makes this passage of Scripture, a parable, so popular?

1. It is relatable. We love seeing the hurts, heartaches, and joys of our own lives played out before us in full drama. Our humanity fully relates to the themes of this parable. We all have experienced the hurt of a rebellious child, the heartache of painful life consequences, and the rejoicing over restored relationships.

2. It is cultural. Few parables immerse the reader in such a deep cultural context as the one we are about to study. In fact, the full impact of this story is lost if we neglect to include the culture to which Christ was speaking. These social cues help us fit the puzzle together and make sense of the intricacies that are described within the text.

3. It is understandable. It was given to be understood. Many of the parables that Jesus used to teach truth also include a brief explanation afterward. He wants the listeners to walk away with an understanding of the symbolism and meaning. After this parable, Jesus simply turns away and begins talking to the disciples. The parable is understandable as it was given.

4. It is teachable. The themes and lessons from this story are easy to learn, understand, and pass on to the next generation of believers. Children of all ages can glean from its truth and walk away with a better understanding of God's unfailing love.

5. It is eternal. The Parable of the Prodigal Son is so much more than just a story. In fact, it is probably one of the most important passages of the entire New Testament! I know that sounds bold....it is meant to be a bold statement. No other passage of Scripture measures up in significance as it relates to mankind and salvation. Why? Because our Savior, the master teacher, carefully crafts this intricate story to explain and reveal detailed truths of salvation; no other writer in the New Testament captures the details of salvation with such clarity.

Not only are there well-known passages of Scripture, there are also well-loved themes. I would dare say that no theme of God's Revelation is as well loved and dear to our hearts as God's plan of salvation for mankind. This story begins in the Garden of Eden; Adam and Eve living in a perfect world, untainted by the stain of sin. Through their disobedience mankind is plunged into the depths of sin. Fellowship has been broken. The heart of man dwells in rebellion toward God. Paul describes this perfectly in Romans 3:10-12 where he states "As it is written, There is none righteous, no, not one: There is none that understandeth, there is none that seeketh after God. They are all gone out of the way, they are together become unprofitable; there is none that doeth good, no, not one."

Every man stands in rebellion to God and separated by spiritual death. With hearts dominated by sin, mankind needed a Savior to free him from sin's grip; enter Jesus Christ! The very God that man rebelled against, lovingly and graciously offers a restored fellowship with God through Jesus Christ. This gift is eternal life and the immediate position of sonship with the Father. As you know, however, no gift is free. It was paid for with the precious blood of Jesus Christ, dying on the cross of Calvary for the sins of all mankind.

This well-loved theme creates its own set of questions. How does a person come to saving faith? How can we be guilty and yet forgiven? Can someone know the truth but not be a believer? How is a sinner drawn to the Father? What does true repentance look like? I'll give you a hint...

It looks just like the Parable of the Prodigal Son!

Chapter 1
Soteriology: The Defining Issue

After my junior year of high school I had the privilege of traveling with our youth group from South Carolina to Colorado. I use the word 'privilege' with utmost reluctance; I don't think I added much to that trip, but I was surrounded by some very special spiritual mentors that invested heavily in my life. To make the trip bearable, we took out many of the back seats of the bus and had areas where cots were set up for sleeping, storage for suitcases, and folding chairs. It was quite the setup! Late in the evening we would fill up with fuel and with maps in hand, would drive through the night. I often had the opportunity to sit up front with our driver and help him 'navigate' through the night as we made our way out west. Before we would head off for the night, I would ask our driver, Mr. Houk, where we were headed. I wanted to know our destination. Knowing your destination makes the journey a little less strenuous; road signs make more sense when you know where you are going.

Where are we going with this book? Well, our destination is simple; we want to understand more about salvation by studying the words of Jesus Christ. Along the way there are some lane changes, a few roadblocks, and we will constantly glance down at the map to make sure we are still on course. The journey from South Carolina to Colorado took days and many miles; the journey through the Parable of the Prodigal Son is long as well. By the end of our trip we will have addressed a critical issue that will likely define our generation of Christians and affect our churches for years to come.

What issue will define our generation of believers?

All through church history, each generation of believers has faced unique issues and circumstances that have tested their resolve. No generation has been exempt. Some have faced the fires of persecution while others have dared to stand for sound doctrine. The early church and its descendants suffered greatly at the hands of Roman persecutors; Christians were blamed for political issues, natural disasters, as well as acts of terrorism. The blood of those early martyrs watered the seed of the gospel and history records an exponential growth of Christianity; real faith is the most attractive result of the true gospel! However, with the "conversion" of the Roman Emperor Constantine, all that changed, and Christianity was brought into the open. In fact, 'everyone' became a Christian; it was then the official religion of the Roman Empire. History records that this shift toward universal Christianity had devastating effects on the purity of the church. Mass conversions and rapid growth quickly altered the face of Christianity and sent it down a difficult path.

History has recorded the pathway that the church followed; it is littered with heresy, cults, false teaching, and controversy. The earliest post-Acts believers were focused on establishing the canon of Scripture and accurately defining the wording of theology through the creeds and apologetics. Soon though, attacks on sound doctrine surfaced through errant philosophy; issues such as the Trinity, the deity and nature of Christ, allegiance to the law, and controversy surrounding paintings as idols marked the early church. The doctrine of soteriology was not immune from those attacks. It was in this era that we saw the rise of variant teachings in regards to the sinfulness of man and his untainted moral will. The church pushed back on these heresies; however, in an effort to bring the pendulum back to center, the church overshot sound doctrine and shifted quickly toward the establishment of extra-Biblical church traditions. This was the beginning of the Catholic Church and its religious dominance. Men thought it necessary to set up religious hierarchy to address heretical teachings with the eventual establishment of the pope and his infallible authority over religious affairs.

For many generations true Christianity was held hostage to organized religion. From Constantine's turn toward faith (312 AD) until the 1500's, believers were regularly persecuted for their faith and stands against the Catholic Church. Many faithful believers were martyred for their faith and refusal to embrace Catholicism; they were the ones labeled heretics. During this time, the availability of the Scriptures to the common man was of paramount importance. Men like John Wycliffe, William Tyndale and John Huss gave their lives for the glorious cause of their day: the translation and propagation of the Scriptures. In more modern times, the 1900s were filled with there own share of movements that would stray from a traditional interpretation of Scripture and move toward false gospels. Americanism, Mormonism, Jehovah's Witness, Modernism, Prosperity Theology, the modern tongues movement; each of these creates it's own fundamental framework for salvation by altering in some form the true Gospel while attempting to lay claim to 'true Christianity.'

Our generation as well must face theological challenges. Within Baptist circles, one of the most defining issues that we see in the body of Christ today surrounds the relationship between man's responsibility and God's sovereignty in salvation. There is no getting around this issue as the defining theological divide that occurs among seminaries, colleges, pastors, missionaries, churches and believers in our generation. This issue creates groups within the body of Christ that are defined solely by their position on this issue. If a pastor is in agreement with a local pastors' fellowship, he is welcomed into the 'camp,' and there is mutual support and camaraderie. If that pastor is in disagreement, he is quickly labeled and categorized by that belief. I know there are exceptions to this practice, but it is easy to see that modern Christianity is pretty clearly divided and defined along this one issue. Simply put, this is the issue that will define our generation of believers.

That disagreement is not the focus of this book but stands as the backdrop to our study. It is impossible to study a passage of Scripture that deals with salvation without addressing in some way the sovereignty of God, man's depravity, God's grace and the beauty of heart repentance. In fact, the very existence of this book will be confusing or offensive to some. There are those that would challenge the conclusion that this parable speaks of salvation at all. Our goal is not to define our understanding of salvation and force this passage into it, but rather to allow the words of Jesus to better inform our understanding of His plan of redemption. So to better understand where our study will take us, we need to first consider the different positions on salvation.

Three Views on Salvation

The conversation surrounding God's sovereignty and man's responsibility in salvation usually assumes a binary division, one side lifting up man's free will and the other championing God's sovereign control. The historical names that inevitably emerge in that discussion are Pelagius and Augustine. Those on each side often make presumptions of the other and claim to have the theological high ground. Please understand that there is variance even within the groups, and there are varying degrees to which people hold to their soteriological doctrines. However, there are actually three historic positions that have shaped this soteriological discussion.

The first group, and often the one that is overlooked in heated discussions, is what we will call the 'Traditional View' of soteriology. It is 'traditional' in that it was the predominant view of the earliest church fathers. Though the Augustinian and Pelagian views have received the most historical notoriety (we will discuss them in a moment), the earliest beliefs on man's freedom to accept the offer of redemption appear to be the closest to the Apostolic tradition and are documented well before Pelagius and Augustine lived. Theologians such as Ignatius, Justin Martyr, Irenaeus, Tertullian and many others held to this position: they affirmed the balance between God's transcendence over creation with the necessity of man's response to the gospel. Consider the clear words of these theologians.

> -Seeing, then, all thing have an end, and there is set before us life upon our observance, but death as the result of disobedience, and every one, according to the choice that he makes, shall go to his own place, let us flee from death, and make choice of life.[1] -Ignatius

> -We have learned from the prophets, and we hold it to be true, that punishments, and chastisements, and good rewards, are rendered according to the merit of each man's actions.

---

[1] Ignatius, *The Epistle of Agnatius* (London: Aeterna Press, 2016), 61. Accessed through google books 02/15/2018.

Since if it be not so, but all things happen by fate, neither is anything at all in our own power. For if it be fated that this man, e.g., be good, and this other evil, neither is the former meritorious nor the latter to be blamed. And again, unless the human race have the power of avoiding evil and choosing good by free choice, they are not accountable for their actions, of whatever kind they be.[2] -Justin Martyr

-This expression [of our Lord], "How often would I have gathered thy children together, and thou wouldest not," set forth the ancient law of human liberty, because God made man a free [agent] from the beginning, possessing his own power, even as he does his own soul, to obey the behests (ad utendum sententia) of God voluntarily, and not by compulsion of God.[3] -Irenaeus

-This also is clearly defined in the teaching of the Church, that every rational soul is possessed of free-will and volition;[4] -Origen

-I find, then, that man was by God constituted free, master of his own will and power; indicating the presence of God's image and likeness in him by nothing so well as by this

---

[2] Justin Martyr, *Translations of the Writings of the Fathers Volume II Justin Martyr* (Edinburgh, T and T Clark: 1868), 43. Accessed through google books 02/15/2018.

[3] Irenaeus, *Translations of the Writings of the Fathers Volume IX Irenaeus* (Edinburgh, T and T Clark: 1869), 37. Accessed through google books 02/15/2018.

[4] Origen, *The Writings of Origen* (Edinburgh, T and T Clark: 1869), 4. Accessed through google books 02/15/2018.

constitution of his nature.[5] -Tertullian

These early theologians, a mere generation or two removed from the apostles themselves, struck a balance in their soteriology that lifted up Christ as the sole mover in salvation and yet recognized that it was God's authority as transcendent Creator that granted to man the freedom to accept that gracious call to repent. In fact, their theology and writings became the foundation on which future theology was built.

The second view we will examine was championed by a British monk, Pelagius, who affirmed in his theology that Adam's original sin did not taint human nature and that mankind maintained a mortal will that was able to choose good or evil apart from any work of the Holy Spirit. In his travels, he was exposed to those claiming the name of Christ and yet living in sin and debauchery. In his desire to "protect" the character of God, he "put the responsibility for avoiding sin back on individuals by making it a matter of each person's choice whether to sin, not a matter of what grace God gave or did not give."[6] Pelagius concluded that man was born free from sin and that he only became a sinner through his own free-will choice. In essence, he taught that man was born with a sinless nature. For those that understand what Scripture says about sin and our

---

[5] Alexander Roberts and James Donaldson, *The Ante-Nicene Fathers Vol. III* (New York, Scribner's Sons: 1903), 301. Accessed through google books 02/15/2018.

[6] Janine Ungvarsky, *Pelagius* (Ipswich, MA, Salem Press: 2016) no page. Accessed online 02/24/18 through ebscohost.com

human nature, it will come as no surprise that Pelagius's soteriology was denounced as heresy. The most vocal objector was a theologian named Augustine. He was the architect of the third view we will consider.

Augustine was born in the mid 300's and was a contemporary to Pelagius. His early years were spent in deep immorality and spiritual wanderings. He wrote in *Confessions* that his sinful living drove him toward religious experience and into the teachings of Manichaeism; this religious system rivaled Christianity and proposed a framework where good and evil (light and darkness...spiritual and material) are fixed in an earthly struggle.[7] This early philosophical framework cast a dark shadow on Augustine's view of man's nature and shaped his future understanding of man's will. Augustine also embraced a hermeneutic model that espoused the allegorization of Scripture; his rejection of literal interpretation led to a dependence on the church for Scriptural understanding and eventually landed on the authority of church tradition over Scriptural context.[8] Sadly, this theological shift led him far away from the earliest church positions and eventually established his theology as a foundation on which the Roman Catholicism is built.[9]

---

[7] Louis Berkof, *The History of Christian Doctrine* (Peoria, IL: Banner of Truth, 2015), 131.

[8] Ron Bigalke, "Historical Survey of Biblical Interpretation," *Journal of Dispensational Theology* 14:42 (2010): 42.

[9] John Walvoord, Millennial Series Part 7: Amillennial Soteriology," *Bibliotheca Sacra* 107:427 (1950): 282.

Most importantly, in a response to Pelagius and with the desire to 'defend' the character of God, Augustine shifted his soteriology as far from Pelagius's heresy as possible to the point of denying that man has any ability to respond to the gospel; man is unable to respond at all to the call of God in salvation. This change from early church theology required that other long held doctrines had to be altered as well to fit within this framework. Instead of a free offer of the gospel to all mankind, he proposed that only those chosen for redemption could be saved; all others were chosen for damnation.[10] He taught that God could, as a result of his sovereignty, take away salvation from a Christian if he so desired. He developed the concept of purgatory to accomodate for those who had lost their salvation yet were still ordained to eternal life.[11] Excluding Pelagius, whose teachings are still considered heretical by most, we see that the traditional position and Augustine's position became the two predominant modes by which salvation was taught.

Skip ahead about a thousand years. These two positions remained the two dominant positions and were further described by two theologians that lived in the 1500s: John Calvin and Jacobus Arminius. These two men, though not actually ministering at the same time, were actually more alike in their theology than you might think. Typically they are

---

[10] Berkof, 136.

[11] David Anderson, "The Soteriological Impact of Augustine's Change from Premillennialism to Amillennialism," *Journal of Grace Evangelical Society* 15 (2002): 33.

portrayed as theological antagonists, sparing over their differences in theological circles. In reality, they were both firm adherants to the five solas of the reformation, agreed on the doctrine of original sin, and agreed on the penal-substitutionary view of atonement. Arminius went so far as to say that...

> "I affirm that in the interpretation of the Scriptures Calvin is incomparable, and that his Commentaries are more to be valued than anything that is handed down to us in the writings of the Fathers—so much so that I concede to him a certain spirit of prophecy in which he stands distinguished above others, above most, indeed, above all." -Jacobus Arminius[12]

There was one area, though, that Arminius believed that John Calvin had strayed from proper Biblical interpretation: Calvin's five points of soteriology (total depravity, unconditional election, limited atonement, irresistable grace, and preservation of the saints). Though not all who hold to Calvinism would concur with all five, the overarching theme of that soteriological position is that God's sovereignty is the single determining factor in history, both political and spiritual. Nothing happens apart from God's sovereign control. From a Calvinist's perspective, this position lifts God above all and therefore exalts him as truly sovereign. This standpoint does not recognize that man has a free will but rather he is so dead in his sin that he is incapable of belief, faith, or repentance.

---

[12] Arminius; cited in Bangs, "Arminius As a Reformed Theologian," 216; cited in Pinson, "Will the Real Arminius Please Stand Up?," 123.

God's sovereign choosing alone determines who will come to faith and who will be damned for eternity. In summary, Calvinism seeks to exalt the sovereignty of God and denies the free will of man.

It is time to compare!

It might be helpful for us to contrast the two positions side by side. This allows us to see an apples to apples comparison between the two models; this will also give us a baseline by which to analyze and apply these positions to the passage that we are studying...to see which matches with Christ's teachings. Let us consider the following six areas of contrast.

God's Sovereignty

> **Calvinism**: God's sovereignty is absolute. All things are determined by His will. Nothing occurs that is not foreordained by His eternal will.
>
> **Arminianism**: God's sovereignty is absolute. Within His sovereignty God grants to man a will to respond to the gospel. He can do so because He is sovereign.

Man's Depravity

> **Calvinism**: Man is depraved. He is unable to respond to the gospel call and cannot believe apart from God's regeneration first.
>
> **Arminianism**: Man is depraved. Every part of his being is affected by his sin nature. Man, in his sin, cannot just

choose to come to God. However, when the Holy Spirit draws through his Word, man can either submit to that drawing or reject it.

Election

Calvinism: Before the foundation of the world, God unconditionally chose some to be redeemed and others to be damned. Only the elect have been chosen for salvation.

Arminianism: Election is based on God's foreknowledge of those that would accept His offer of grace. The saved are part of the elect; they are not elected to salvation but rather to walk in Christ.

Christ's Atonement

Calvinism: Jesus Christ died to only save those that are the elect. His blood was not shed for those damned to hell. His atonement was limited in scope to only those who He chose to be saved.

Arminianism: Jesus Christ died for all mankind. Jesus's death provided the way and the means for all people to be saved by faith.

Grace

Calvinism: God's salvific grace is irresistable. If a person is one of the elect (chosen for salvation), then God's grace will draw that sinner to salvation.

Arminianism: God's offer of grace is to all men. Through the drawing of the Spirit, man can respond to that grace through acceptance or rejection.

Man's Will

> **Calvinism**: Man's depravity extends to every part of man, making him incapable of responding to the moving of the Holy Spirit.
>
> **Arminianism**: Man's depravity extends to every part of man; however, God has granted to man the ability to respond to His call of salvation.

No doubt, you have an opinion on the matter even as you read through that comparison, and that's a wonderful thing! My goal with this book isn't to try to make the Scriptures line up with one or the other but to allow the words of Christ to tell us where our theology of salvation should fall. Isn't that what an exegetical study should do? I give you my word that I will take great care to expose the truths of Scripture in regards to this passage. Will you in turn pledge that you will allow God's Word to guide your theology of salvation?

Chapter 2
Why Parables?

Now that we have established the value of a study on salvation, we should just dive right into the parable...right? If you are like me, you like to get right to it! That would be a legitimate option, and I'm sure many good books have jumped right to the passage in the first chapter. I would like us to take a different approach as we look at this wonderful parable. Instead of jumping right in, we are going to establish the foundation on which this parable is built; doing so will help us to understand the intricacies and cultural dynamics that could easily be overlooked. Do you really want to know what Jesus was communicating through His words? Is your desire to understand the deep and wonderful meaning of the text? To really understand the Parable of the Prodigal Son to its fullest, we need to ask a few questions, and consider the answers.

Question #1

So our first question is "What is a parable? At some point in your life you have probably heard it described as "an earthly story with a heavenly meaning." When describing the most influential form of rhetoric that Jesus used on earth, it seems that this definition isn't quite sufficient to really bear the weight of the moment. However, before we dismiss this definition as too simplistic, we should recognize that it does contain two important truths that help define a parable.

First, a parable is an earthly story. No matter how simplistic or complex, there is an earthly quality to parables that makes them understandable and relatable. Second, a parable has a heavenly meaning. Jesus Christ did not speak in parables to reveal earthly truth; He used that literary device to also reveal spiritual truths.

The 'earthly' and 'heavenly' parts to a parable are forever linked in God's Revelation. To understand the 'heavenly' you must study and consider how the 'earthly' portion is being presented and used within the text. Consequently, if we understand the 'heavenly' aspect of a parable, we can then use that spiritual knowledge to help us learn and understand the 'earthly' parts that may be a historical mystery within our culture.

The English word *parable* is actually a transliteration from the Greek. In other words, we borrowed it. Actually, we took the Greek word and simply made it into an English word by adjusting the pronunciation. The Greek root word at hand is *paraballo* which means "to throw alongside and compare." *Para* meaning "with or along" and *ballo* meaning "to throw." Literally, parables are a way to teach truth by throwing an illustration and story alongside the spiritual truth to make it more clear.

While we are familiar with the word *parable* in a Scriptural context, this literary device is as effective with secular truths as well! Consider the collection of uninspired yet morally profound parables called "Aesop's Fables." Though little is know of "Aesop the Fable Writer," historians place this Greek poet's existence in the 5th Century BC.[13] Born a slave, he was rewarded with freedom as a result of his intense desire to learn and understand truth.[14] Upon receiving his freedom, he travelled abroad and studied underneath some of the greatest philosophers and learned men of his day. In an attempt to pass on his wisdom to others, he thought it best to wrap truth in the garments of a simple story. Initially, his parables were not written but handed down orally; over the generations they were recorded, and his fame as a purveyor of truth and wisdom was secured in time. The popularity of Aesop's parables, as well as all the fables attributed to him, stem from their simplistic earthly truth that teach a deeper yet profound moral pattern.

No doubt you have heard Aesop's story of "The Ant and the Grasshopper." One day a grasshopper was jumping around in the field and came across an ant that was working with great determination. The Grasshopper said, "Why are you working so hard...the air is warm and the sun is shining. Why don't you

---

[13] "The Histories of Herodotus of Halicarnassus. trans. George Rawlinson, Book I, p.132 Archived August 19, 2006, at the Wayback Machine.
[14] http://www.aesopfables.com/cgi/aesop1.cgi?1&LifeofAesop. (Accessed 04/02/2018)

come relax with me for a while?" The Ant replied, "I can't. I am putting up the food for the winter. If you were wise you would do the same!" The Grasshopper responded sarcastically, "Why should I worry about the winter? I have plenty of time." Of course, when the winter winds were blowing and Grasshopper was hungry, he looked over and saw the ants handing out their daily food stores. What did Grasshopper learn? Prepare ahead of time for the times of need. This parable teaches a simple yet profound truth that is best learned through the events that unfold between a grasshopper and an ant. In fact, you would struggle to teach that truth in a more profound way than through the vehicle of a simple story.

In the same way, parables in Scripture are just a vehicle to teach an important truth. Christ spoke in parables often and used them to effectively communicate spiritual truths. Consider the following principles that Jesus Christ chose to teach through the vehicle of parables:

- There will be many responses to the gospel. - Parable of the Sower
- The Kingdom of God starts small but grows quickly. - Parable of the Leaven
- There is rejoicing in Heaven over a saved soul. - Parable of the Lost Coin
- We are commanded to love our neighbor. -Parable of the Good Samaritan
- We are commanded to forgive each other. - Parable of

the Unforgiving Servant
- God cares about our needs. - Parable of the Friend at Night
- God will separate out the true believers from the frauds. - Parable of the Tares
- We are to influence our communities. - Parable of the Lamp and Bushel
- Believers are to use their talents to further the kingdom. - Parable of the Talents
- Don't compare yourself to others. - Parable of the Pharisee and Publican.

The list could go on. The three synoptic gospels (Matthew, Mark, and Luke) contain the traditional parables of Christ while John recorded the allegorical statements that Christ made (the vine, the door, the bread of life, the shepherd...). Matthew contains 23 parables, Mark 8, but the book of Luke has the most recorded with 24, 18 of which are unique to that book. It is right in the middle of Luke's gospel that we find the Parable of the Prodigal Son.

Question #2

What was the purpose of New Testament parables? Let's begin to answer this question by restating our previous definition. A parable is an "earthly story with a heavenly meaning." Growing up I heard this description often. Maybe too often. It became so engrained in my conscience that whenever someone asks about a parable today it becomes my first reaction. As it was said before, it is not a bad definition; it does, however, cause some confusion about parables. It creates a misunderstanding of purpose in that it seems to tell us that parables served only one purpose.

Why did Jesus use parables? I have asked teenagers this question as a youth pastor. I have asked junior age kids as a camp speaker. I have asked adults this question as a senior pastor. The overwhelming answer that I hear is that parables were used to help teach spiritual truth. I don't recall a single time where I have called on a person to answer that question, and the answer was not a variation of that in some shape or form.

Purpose #1 - To Reveal Truth

Well, the first purpose of parables was, indeed, to teach spiritual truth. In fact, Jesus used parables to reveal truth that would be hard to understand or comprehend otherwise. Consider these parables that Christ used to teach truth to the listeners.
- Parable of the Mustard Seed - reveals the small beginnings of a growing kingdom
- Parable of the Sower - reveals the different responses that the heart has to the gospel

- Parable of Hidden Treasure - reveals the true value of the kingdom
- Parable of Wheat and Tares - reveals how God will separate true believers from false converts
- Parable of the Good Samaritan - reveals the heart of God in regards to loving our neighbor
- Parable of Unmerciful Servant - reveals what a true heart of forgiveness should look like
- Parable of the Talents - reveals the principle of stewardship
- Parable of the Rich Fool - reveals what should be considered valuable
- Parable of the Ten Virgins - reveals the finality of eternity and man's acceptance or rejection

The list could go on. In fact, for every parable that Jesus gave He had a very important spiritual lesson that He wanted to reveal. The very nature of the parables used helps us to not only understand a spiritual truth but to comprehend it at a deeper level. We use illustrations in the same way today. Purposed stories are an incredible communication tool that allow our mind to visualize what is being taught, in turn driving the underlying truth deep into our understanding.

In the same way that we are trying to better understand the purpose of Christ's parables, the disciples found themselves asking the same question. Let's consider the interaction between Jesus, the disciples, and the multitudes in Luke 8:1-10.

The passage tells us that one day Jesus went for a walk with His disciples and ministered to the multitudes. No sooner had He begun and a mass of people surround Him, longing to hear His words and see His miracles. Understanding the opportunity to speak to the people, He positioned himself to be heard. He waited till the people quieted. He spoke.

"A sower went out to sow his seed: and as he sowed, some fell by the way side; and it was trodden down, and the fowls of the air devoured it. And some fell upon a rock; and as soon as it was sprung up, it withered away, because it lacked moisture. And some fell among thorns; and the thorns sprang up with it, and choked it. 8 And other fell on good ground, and sprang up, and bare fruit an hundredfold...He that hath ears to hear, let him hear." Luke 18

Think about those words...let them really sink in. What do you think Jesus was trying to communicate? The disciples were intrigued. Why did Jesus use so many parables? They were always around Him when He taught, and no one on earth knew more about His teaching style and mannerisms. Curious, the disciples asked the question, "What might this parable be?" The Matthew 13 account of the same event records the question a little differently, "Why speakest thou unto them in parables?" Wow! What a great question! In fact, that is the same question we are asking today. Jesus, why did you choose to use parables when you spoke to the multitudes. Here is Christ's reply in the Gospel of Luke.

"And he said, Unto you it is given to know the mysteries of the kingdom of God: but to others in parables; that seeing they might not see, and hearing they might not understand.

Purpose #2 - To Conceal Truth

Did you catch it? In this verse Jesus reveals the second purpose of parables...to hide spiritual truth. Now that may seem foreign to you. In fact, it may have even shocked you to read that Jesus spoke in parables to hide the truth of the Gospel from those whose hearts were hardened. It seems antithetical to the gospel that Jesus Christ would preach truth but would do it in a way to hide that truth from the religious leaders that opposed Him! Didn't they need to hear the gospel? Weren't they in need of heart-changing faith? The answers to both are 'yes.' In fact, we know of at least three members of the religious ruling system that did come to saving faith. Do you know who they are?

The first convert is Nidocemus, the ruler that came to Jesus by night in John 3. We see him quietly coming to Jesus after dark, so as to not be seen and then asking questions concerning spiritual re-birth. After the John 3 conversation, Nicodemus fades from view and is almost forgotten in John's narrative....until Jesus is being taken down from the cross. There we see Nicodemus bringing burial spices and reverently helping take our Lord from off the cross of crucifixion.

Nicodemus wasn't alone that day. He worked quietly alongside Joseph of Arimathaea. Very little is know of this man except for a few verses that reveal his identity in the latter parts of each of the Gospels. Joseph was a rich man, was part of the council that called for Jesus's crucifixion, and is described as a good and righteous man in Luke's gospel. Mark's account gives one more very important piece of information that helps us understand Joseph's motives that day.

"Joseph of Arimathaea, an honourable counsellor, which also waited for the kingdom of God, came, and went in boldly unto Pilate, and craved the body of Jesus."

Where were the disciples? Where was Peter? Where was Matthew? Where was John? They were nowhere to be found. I find it incredibly ironic that the two men that took Christ's body down, wrapped him gently in new burial clothes, lovingly anointed him with spices for burial, and laid him respectfully in the tomb were two men who had once opposed Christ's ministry.

The third and most well known example of a Pharisee's conversion is the Apostle Paul. Paul explains the significance of his religious Jewish upbringing in Philippians 3. Raised in a law abiding Jewish home, Paul (Saul) was proud of his lineage and was a zealous defender of Judaism. His zeal took him into the houses and assemblies of those that followed Christ's teachings; he proudly arrested them and caused a great stir among the

Christian community. This all changed, however, when Jesus appeared to him while on the road to Damascus. This unique salvation experience changed his life; Paul went from the most zealous persecutor of Christians to one of the greatest human influences in the spread of the Gospel.

Nicodemus, Joseph of Arimathaea, and Paul....All three were part of the organized religious leadership that Jesus was speaking to that day.

Yes, the second purpose of parables was to conceal the truth, but it wasn't to conceal it from those that were searching. Rather, it was to conceal it from those with a heart already set against the Son of Man. Consider Christ's words in Matthew 13.

> "For this people's heart is waxed gross, and their ears are dull of hearing, and their eyes they have closed; lest at any time they should see with their eyes, and hear with their ears, and should understand with their heart, and should be converted, and I should heal them. " -
> Matthew 13:15

Jesus is very clear on the progression of the hardening of their heart. It is as follows: the waxing gross of their hearts, the dulling of their ears, and the closing of their eyes. These all prevented the understanding of their heart. Though this passage is sometimes used to demonstrate that Jesus withheld the gospel message to keep them unrepentant, the progression within the text indicates otherwise. To that point, however, consider that particular position and the contradiction it creates within the text.

1. The Pharisees were human, dead in their sin and separate from God.
2. The Pharisees had no power to respond to the Gospel aside from the quickening of the Spirit.
3. Jesus preached the gospel and used parables as a tool of communication.
4. Jesus intentionally used parables to hide the truth of the Gospel from the Pharisees lest they would come to faith.

Not only is that progression missing within the text of Scripture, it is illogical as well. Why would Jesus have to use parables to hide the Gospel from people that had no ability to respond in the first place? Why would you hide the keys from a person that is blind? Instead, we see Jesus using parables to conceal the truth of the Gospel from those that were already living in rejection. What we do find in Scripture are two types of hardening. Self-hardening occurs when the sinful heart of man dwells so long in the sinful mire of rebellion and wickedness that the heart becomes calloused to all that is good. (Exodus 9:34-35, II Chronicles 36:13, Daniel 5:20, Ephesians 4:18, Hebrews 3:12-15) Judicial-hardening, the other form of hardening, is only seen in a few instances in Scripture. God hardened Pharaoh's heart. God hardened the hearts of the Hivites. Isaiah 6 also tells us that God even hardened the heart of the nation of Israel. In fact, Isaiah's prophecy tells us that because of the rebellion of Israel and the constant rebellion of their will, God would harden their heart so that when the Messiah himself was revealed, they would reject Him! (Isaiah 6:1-10) Do you realize that this is the prophecy that Jesus is quoting in the Matthew passage we just read? Jesus is telling his disciples that the concealing of the gospel message through the parables is a fulfillment of prophecy; parables were meant to reveal as well as to conceal truth.

As we finish our general thoughts on parables, consider the effectiveness of parables in Scripture as a vehicle for truth. Do you remember Nathan the prophet's interaction with David that ended with "Thou art the man."? It was a parable that Nathan used to confront David that day about his sin with Bathsheba. It was a parable of a potter and clay that Jeremiah used to illustrate God's authority over Israel. Solomon uses many smaller parables to illustrate the dangerous consequences of sin in the book of Proverbs. Jesus Himself spoke around 40 parables during His earthly ministry and used them quite effectively!

Remember, a parable is an earthly story that is 'cast alongside' a spiritual truth to help us in our understanding. If we neglect either part of the parable (the earthly or spiritual), we are in danger of missing out on the truth that God wants to reveal!

Question #3

Before we begin our venture into Luke 15 we must ask one more very serious question. Without a doubt it is the single most important question that we must consider before journeying into the realm of Scriptural interpretation. In fact, as I write this paragraph my heart is gripped with the seriousness of the moment, and my typing has slowed. The question is simple yet incredibly complex. Is a theological study of a parable even appropriate?

Over the course of my preparation and study for this project, I have had conversations surrounding the appropriateness of any form of theological study from the parables. These were 'iron sharpening iron' moments that helped to keep me focused on the seriousness of the task at hand but also revealed a response that some might have to taking Christ's Parable of the Prodigal Son and drawing soteriological conclusions. I am thankful for those brothers in Christ that are concerned when a passage that is not intended for doctrine is used as foundation for doctrine. Truthfully, that practice can lead to false doctrine very quickly. I share their concern.

Knowing the purpose of parables and why they were used by Christ, we would agree that the normal process of interpretating parables should typically lend itself to a simple explanation and no more. Can you write a book on the Parable of the Mustard Seed? That short illustration is one sentence comprised of around 50 words. How about the Parable of the Pearl of Great Price? Again, one sentence of about 35 words. What about other 'major' parables? We often see the Parable of the Good Samaritan analyzed deeply; it comprises 6 verses and about 165 words. I have never heard opposition giving meaning of the identity of the Levite, the Priest, and the Samaritan in that story. Though there is one clear intent, to establish the identity of the neighbor, there are other evident truths wrapped into that 165 word illustration.

And then we must consider our passage. The Parable of the Prodigal Son is part of three parables given in unison. They account for 28 verses of Scripture, almost 700 words of English text, and close to 500 words in the Greek. They have a unified theme with clear explanation given directly from our Lord within the text itself! To say that there is only one truth to be drawn from this text is to say that our Savior spent a lot of time giving words that didn't matter. Consider these four reasons why a soteriological study from these parables is completely appropriate.

First, it is appropriate to carry out a deeper study of this passage because Christ offers three separate parables that each have an almost identical story and focus. Our Lord used from forty to forty-five distinctly different parables during His earthly teaching ministry. Many of the parables were given in series with a similar focus. Matthew 13 itself contains eight different parables that each center around the kingdom, planting, harvest, weeds, and hidden treasure. Though they were given around a central theme, they are each distinct and reveal a different truth in regards to the kingdom of God. The passage we are studying is special. Jesus gives three parables that are parallel versions with identical language, meaning, and interpretation. The significance of this 'trilogy' within the parables cannot be overlooked in importance. Jesus clearly intended that these be interpreted together and sought to communicate a very important truth as is evidenced by the repetition.

Second, the Parable of the Prodigal Son has deep cultural connections within the text that are wasted breath if we choose to ignore them. The first two (of the three) set up the overall perspective of our interpretation. "Likewise joy shall be in heaven over one sinner that repenteth." (Luke 15:7) "Likewise, I say unto you, there is joy in the presence of the angels of God over one sinner that repenteth." (Luke 15:10) These parables are relatively short but set the stage for the third by telling us where we are headed. Interestingly, Jesus never gives an explanatory statement on the third parable because it's meaning is wrapped up in the statements already given. The third parable is distinctly different than the previous two. It drives the listener deep into the cultural connections of the day and ties the message of salvation directly into the storyline of rebellion, repentance, and redemption.

Third and most important, the context of Christ's words clearly directs us to a conversation on salvation. (I know I may lose a few readers on this point; I ask you to hold on until we get to the exegetical study of the text. Just because we disagree now doesn't mean that God can't use His Word to be a blessing as you continue to read!) For those that don't know, there is a considerable number within Christianity (even among baptists/fundamentalists) that reject the soteriological focus of this passage. Why? Because to accept that Jesus is describing salvation in this passage puts their theological views at odds with Christ's teaching. I don't say this harshly, just as a matter of fact. If, in fact, Christ is describing salvation through this parable, then His teaching stands at odds with the Calvinistic view of total inability, limited atonement, unconditional election, and irresistible grace. A person that holds to these views categorically cannot accept Christ's teaching as soteriological. Please understand, I am not writing this book to try to convince you of my position. I just ask that you allow the Holy Spirit to lead you through the Scriptures as we study them together.

Simply put, there is no way around the overwhelming use of soteriological language within all three of the parables. Consider the following examples directly from the texts:

- The ninety and nine safe versus the one that is lost
- Ninety and nine just persons which need no repentance
- Joy in heaven over a sinner that repents
- Joy in the presence of the angels of God over one sinner that repenteth.
- Father, I have sinned

- My son was lost, and is found
- For this my son was dead, and is alive again

If Christ went to such lengths to give such a detailed picture of salvation using clear soteriological language, I think it is appropriate for us to study this parable and to glean from the words that our Savior spoke in that context. We aren't being irresponsible to take an in-depth look at this parable; it is fitting and proper for us to discover the truths that He skillfully wrapped up in its words!

Chapter 3
Scriptural Context

Now that we understand why parables were used in Scripture, it is time for us to move a little closer to our study of The Parable of the Prodigal Son. If we jump right into the passage, however, without considering the context in which it was given, we run the very grave risk of either misinterpreting Scripture or misapplying truths from the passage. And so much is at stake. At the very core of this parable is a beautiful illustration of the good news of salvation; failure to interpret the parable correctly will cast error into the proper understanding. I hope your desire is to understand what Jesus intended to communicate as much as I do! With that in mind, we must spend a few pages understanding the Scriptural context as well as the cultural context in which we find this passage of Scripture.

Our journey into this passage actually begins at the beginning of Luke chapter 15. It is here that we see Jesus walking and ministering among his favorite group of people:

those that need spiritual renewal! Isn't it interesting that those that had the most knowledge and understanding of the prophecies were the least likely to listen to Christ while those that were the worst of society and outcasts were drawn to him? We see this all throughout the ministry of Christ, from his first day of teaching right up to his last breath. Jesus loved being around sinners!

Just a few chapters later in Luke's gospel account we see Jesus making His way through Jericho. Up in a Sycamore tree, waiting for Jesus to pass, was one of the most hated sinners in all the land: a Jewish tax collector. These Jewish men had given their loyalties to the Roman government and used their appointed power over the people to manipulate and steal. They were dirty thieves. No one liked the tax collectors. When Jesus saw Zaccheus up in the tree, He immediately motioned for him to come down; they went to Zaccheus's house and ate. Though we don't really know what was said to Zaccheus that day, we know that he was a changed man! After that meal with Jesus, Zaccheus took his small personal fortune and began dividing it out among all the people from whom he had stolen; he restored their money four fold!

In this same passage we see the Pharisee's reaction to this encounter with the Savior. "And when they saw it, they all murmured, saying, That he was gone to be guest with a man that is a sinner." (Luke 19:7) Jesus meets with Zaccheus (a man that is a sinner and needs salvation), he is transformed by the gospel message, and the Pharisees complain! This pattern repeats itself all throughout the Gospels; at least 8 times we read that the Pharisees were upset because Jesus was interacting with sinners. They were genuinely bothered that Jesus would offer grace to people so undeserving.

This is the standard reaction of the Pharisees in the Gospels, and this is the foundation on which our parable is built. Luke 15:1-2 states, "Then drew near unto him all the publicans and sinners for to hear him. And the Pharisees and scribes murmured, saying, This man receiveth sinners, and eateth with them." As Jesus was speaking to the multitudes a great number of them gathered around to hear His teachings. The Pharisees became angry. In response, Jesus addressed them.

Christ addresses the Pharisees through three parables: The Parable of the Lost Sheep, The Parable of the Lost Coin, and the Parable of the Lost Son. There is incredible parallelism between these three because they were given to the same group of people to communicate the same eternal truth. In fact, one of the greatest guides to help us understand the Parable of the Prodigal Son (The Parable of the Lost Son) is our understanding of the previous two parables.

The Parable of the Lost Sheep is the first in the trilogy of parables. It is very simple yet teaches a exceedingly clear truth through a story of a sheep and shepherd. Let's look at Luke 15:4-7.

4 What man of you, having an hundred sheep, if he lose one of them, doth not leave the ninety and nine in the wilderness, and go after that which is lost, until he find it? 5 And when he hath found it, he layeth it on his shoulders, rejoicing. 6 And when he cometh home, he calleth together his friends and neighbours, saying unto them, Rejoice with me; for I have found my sheep which was lost. 7 I say unto you, that likewise joy shall be in heaven over one sinner that repenteth, more than over ninety and nine just persons, which need no repentance.

I would like for you to notice a few things about this short parable. First, something was lost. Second, something was found. Third, there was great rejoicing. In just a few concise words, Jesus laid out an easy to understand illustration that reveals a pathway to understand all three of the parables. Lost. Found. Rejoicing. Jesus then ends this parable with an explanation that exposes the heavenly meaning of this story. When sinners come to repentance there is great joy in heaven! Though Jesus doesn't say it verbally, can you sense the contrast He is presenting between the rejoicing in heaven and the murmuring Pharisees. This contrast will become more evident as we continue.

The Parable of the Lost Coin is the second of the three parables. It describes a very similar story and also includes three very important words. It is found in Luke 15:8-10.

8 Either what woman having ten pieces of silver, if she lose one piece, doth not light a candle, and sweep the house, and seek diligently till she find it? 9 And when she hath found it, she calleth her friends and her neighbours together, saying, Rejoice with me; for I have found the piece which I had lost. 10 Likewise, I say unto you, there is joy in the presence of the angels of God over one sinner that repenteth.

I'm sure you caught the three words: lost, found, and rejoicing! This parable is so similar to the first that it plays out almost identically as the first. Something valuable is lost. That item of great value is found. Everyone gathers around and rejoices. And lest we think that there is a lack of clarity over the rejoicing, Jesus again clarifies that there is likewise rejoicing in heaven when one lost soul comes to repentance.

This is so simple yet so foundational to properly understanding the message of the Parable of the Prodigal Son! These three parables were given as a package deal…you can't interpret one independently of the others. Each one is teaching the exact same principle as the others but from a different earthly perspective. Lost. Found. Rejoicing.

Lost! Something valuable has been lost. It is no longer where it should and it has been separated from the one person that holds it most valuable. Notice that the 'lost' in these parables very clearly teaches separation. There is a lost sheep, a lost coin, and a lost son. The meaning and interpreation of 'lost' cannot change in the third parable or else you are changing the interpretation that Jesus Christ Himself laid out for us to receive.

Found! Something valuable has been found. It has been

brought back to where it should be and is no longer separated from the one person that holds it most valuable. The 'found' in these parables clearly teaches a change in position, from separated to united.

Rejoicing! The central character in each parable rejoices over the found item of value. This will also hold true for all three of the parables. The shepherd rejoiced over the found sheep; the woman rejoiced over the found coin; and the Father rejoiced over the found son. You may be wondering why this is important. Let me explain.

Do you remember the title of this book? Salvation Through the Eyes of the Prodigal Son. Salvation is the clear focus of this parable, and the Scriptural context is central to being confident of that fact. There are some that would forcibly isolate the Parable of the Prodigal Son from the surrounding Scriptural context. As stated before, this is very dangerous because it then allows for interpretations to be forced onto the parable as opposed to letting the parable interpret itself for us. Though the text is clearly about the rejoicing over the lost sinner that repents (salvation) and was given to Pharisees that murmured that Jesus fellowshipped with sinners, some have strayed from that inherent textual interpretation. Instead, the alternative interpretation is that the Parable of the Prodigal Son isn't about salvation at all but rather the wayward behavior of a rebellious Christian. It is about Jesus's unfailing mercy and grace demonsrated to a backslidden believer. While this isn't a bad interpretation and definitely demonstrates the love of the father, is this really what Christ was trying to communicate? God's love to a backslidden believer?

Here are a few questions to consider. Were the Pharisees angry that Jesus was fellowshipping with backslidden believers? Does the lost sheep in Scripture represent a backslidden believer? Does Scripture anywhere indicate that there is "rejoicing in heaven" over a backslidden believer confessing of his sin? Why does the word "lost" connotate a sinful state in other passages yet here indicate a backslider?

Friend, this parable is clearly about salvation! Jesus masterfully crafts a story of a rebellious son and casts it alongside our understanding of salvation to give clarity and perspective. I pray that as you continue reading God will use His word to bring new understanding and appreciation to the great salvation that He offers to all mankind!

Luke 19:10 - For the Son of man is come to seek and to save that which was lost.

Chapter 4
Cultural Context

Recently, I was teaching the Resurrection story to a group of kids in our church. I carefully worked my way through the death of Christ and then to His burial in a borrowed tomb. Intending to keep the kids connected, I began asking a series of questions. "Who took Jesus off the cross?" A child responded, "Joseph!" "Where did they put Jesus's body?" Another piped up, "In the borrowed tomb." Holding the flashcard with the Roman soldiers guarding the door to the tomb, I asked confidently.... "Do you see the soldiers holding the spear? What was the spear for?" Proudly a young boy raised his hand and proclaimed, "For picking up hay!"

Believe it or not, that young man is correct. A spear is for picking up hay, at least in my part of the country. Hay fields, cow pastures, chicken houses, and lots of big tractors....that is what you will see if you come visit our community. Every spring the nearest town hosts a pottery festival that attracts thousands of people; Seagrove, NC is the pottery capitol of the United States! Around May the farmers will get the first cut of hay, weather permitting. Every Tuesday you see trailers hauling cattle to the meat processor, and every Friday they are hauling them to the cattle auction. Chicken farmers sell the 'chicken litter' to the hay farmers, and they spread that dark, rich fertilizer on the fields with giant trucks with spreaders on the back. Entire fields are overtaken by the "brown cloud of death" as that dry fertilizer creates a dense fog of stench that moves along with the breeze. Sounds beautiful, doesn't it? We live in a farming culture.

Culture determines context. In a farming culture, tractors have a giant 'spear' on the front so they can lift the giant rolls of hay. The young man in our story answered the question correctly based on his cultural upbringing. A tractor spear is indeed for picking up hay! Why is this story relevant to our discussion? It demonstrates that the culture that we grow up in absolutely affects how we read and interpret the Scriptures. We wouldn't expect a person to do otherwise! Knowing that truth, it helps us to see the importance of considering the cultural context in which our parable is written.

When Jesus Christ spoke this parable He wasn't standing in a small rural church in central North Carolina. He wasn't speaking to a large crowd assembled at the 'First Baptist Church' of your nearest major city. This wasn't an appearance at a Christian college chapel, a megachurch gathering, or frankly anything that looks like modern American culture. Jesus was speaking to a culture that was very different than ours and gave to them a parable that is riddled with cultural inferences and connections. If we are to understand how this parable reached into their culture and communicated spiritual truth, we first need to understand a few things about the culture to which Jesus is speaking.

For just a few moments, let's consider how our understanding of Biblical culture is critical to understanding the proper context of the Scriptures.

- When Jesus was asked if it was lawful to pay tribute Caesar, He was being asked a question that merged his message of the kingdom with the <u>political</u> atmosphere of the day.
- A proper understanding of the <u>religious</u> customs of the day give better context to the casting out of the money changers.
- The Parable of the Sower was given within a Palestinian <u>agricultural</u> context.
- The <u>clothing</u> of the day was very significant. Ignore the implication of the coat of the overseer and you completely misinterpret the context of Joseph's teenage years.
- An understanding of Biblical <u>geography</u> reveals the proper context of the 'lukewarm' passage in Revelation 3; failure to consider that context results in a very awkward and incorrect interpretation of Christ's words.
- A <u>military</u> context is included in Christ's urging to "go with them twain."

- In Psalm 149 David danced! There was a context of rejoicing that can't be ignored.
- Studying history reveals a better understanding of the timing of the Minor Prophets and helps us see the reality of their message.
- Is diet important? Sure! Paul addresses issues surrounding food, and he especially deals with the intersection of diet and religious practices.
- If you ignore the athletic context of Paul's writings, you can misinterpret his words on the Bema Seat; Paul's context helps us understand his words.
- Understanding the weather patterns around the Sea of Galilee help us visualize and understand the disciples' fear over the fierce storm.
- A proper grasp of servanthood and slavery reveals depth of humility demonstrated when Jesus washed the disciples' feet.

Behavior, patterns of interaction, societal norms, conflict resolution patterns, and even perceived moral values: these only scratch the surface of the human interactions that are contained with a culture. Imagine taking a Biblical story that is grounded in cultural implications and ethics, firmly uprooting it through translation, transporting it to a modern civilization with completely different cultural norms, and then expecting to fully understand the intricasies of the conversation. That is our task with the Parable of the Prodigal Son.

3 General Categories of Global Cultures

Every culture has a driving force. In reality, there are three recognized driving forces that affect all cultures to some degree...some more than others. This generalization produces three basic categories into which global cultures can be divided: guilt cultures, shame cultures, and fear cultures. This is not a new concept, though it may be new to you; it is quite possible that you have never considered the driving forces behind culture. The reality is that you don't know what you don't know! We become so inwardly focused as humans that we fail to see that others may view Scripture from a different cultural perspective. This inward cultural focus often keeps us from a full realization of the power of Biblical narratives and messages.

Guilt Cultures

We will consider this one first because it is the type of culture that most of the readers of this book would be familiar with. Guilt is a strong driving force and tends to drive cultures that are more westernized. In these cultures there is a strong sense of right versus wrong. Many Western societies are built on the concept that when there are two choices; there is a right way and a wrong way. This ingrained cultural force expresses itself in how we perceive and analyze everything around us! We see it played out in our entertainment (there is usually a good character and a bad character), in our food choices (this food is good for you, this food is bad for you), and in how we view laws and restrictions as well. Those that obey the law are good, and those that break the law are bad. It is just the way we think and interpret the world around us.

Alongside the understanding of good versus evil, is the driving force of guilt versus innocence. Because Westerners paint the world with such a black and white brush, the driving force that is created is guilt. Western society loaths guilt. We will do whatever it takes to free ourselves from the guilty conscience that comes from choosing the 'bad' choice in life. Notice how this doesn't keep people from doing wrong, only avoiding the guilt of that wrong decision.

Consider this simple illustration. Hop in the car and come with me as we drive north on I-95 up the east coast. As we near the interstate, we carefully accelerate down the onramp and soon find ourselves ready to merge with the fast-moving traffic. Blinker on. Use the mirrors. We carefully move to the left and are quickly swept away in the steady flow of vehicles. Trying to avoid creating a bottleneck, we move with the flow of traffic.

Now pause the story, and let me ask this question....how fast are we travelling? Without even knowing the speed limit, I would say that we are probably travelling 10-15 miles per hour faster than the posted speed limit. It's likely we are even being passed by cars going much faster! The mass of humanity swiftly cruises right past the speed limit sign with no desire to slow at all....until there is a police cruiser in the left lane.

Now the story changes because no one wants to pass the

police car. No one wants to be found guilty by the local law enforcement. We were all guilty before hand, but we avoided that guilt by convincing ourselves that our speed was necessary. "My meeting is important." "I have better things to do than sit in traffic." "I'm running late." Now that there is someone to hold us accountable, we all slow down to avoid guilt.

The story changes again. The blue lights come alive, and some poor soul is singled out and pulled to the side. But it wasn't us! Whew! Just as soon as the police car is out of sight, the traffic pace picks back up, and we are on our way like nothing happened. Life is good again in the fast lane!

Have you ever noticed that when Westerners begin sharing the gospel message to someone that is not a believer, they inevitably jump to the starting point of guilt? I can think of many prominent methods of Western evangelism that all start at premise that we are guilty before God. Romans 3 is usually the launching point, and man's sin is the focus. If we can just help them see that they are guilty before God then they will see their need of a Savior. This 'guilt-driven' view of culture also affects how we interpret the Scriptures as well as eventually how we apply the Scriptures. However, the Bible wasn't written in a Westernized culture! So if you want to fully understand what Jesus was saying as He gave the Parable of the Prodigal Son, you must recognize the cultural differences.

Fear Cultures

We won't spend much time with this one because it doesn't

affect our conversation as deeply. Fear cultures are predominately found in tribal and jungle cultures of the world. There is an intense connection with the spirit world and a constant fear of upsetting the balance between the forces of good and evil. Whenever there is famine or disease this culture is quick to attempt to bring the spirits back into harmony through sacrifice or spiritual spells. These cultures are driven to appease the spirit forces and live in constant fear that wrong actions will set the spirits in motion to punish them and their village. The cultural measuring stick is fear and power.

Consider how differently a person in this culture would understand and interpret the Scriptures. For just a moment, view the plagues on Egypt through their eyes. Consider how they would understand the parting of the Red Sea, the miracle of tongues at Pentecost, or even the New Testament teaching of the Holy Spirit endwelling. Ministering in a fear based culture must be done with great care and understanding; their cultural perspective demands it!

Shame Cultures

The third and most important cultural force to our study is the honor/shame dynamic that we will see played out in our passage. Just as guilt/innocence and fear/power are driving forces of culture, the tension between honor and shame is the force that stands behind cultural interpretation in ancient and modern middle eastern countries.

Let's try to loosely define some terms. When we speak of

honor, we are talking about the sense of worth that an individual has within the collective group. To have honor is to have value and to be viewed as meeting the social norms of society. In these cultures, honor is by nature communal; a person's worth is based on the appearances within the community group. While guilt/innocence cultures tend to be more individualistic, honor/shame cultures are driven by the community. Decisions are made in relation to how they will affect the community. People in these cultures think more about how they will be perceived by the community around them. The community means everything.

Does that mean that honor/shame cultures have no sense of right or wrong? Absolutely not. Honor/shame cultures have a clear sense of morality that is often very clearly defined for those in the community, though the moral code is often unwritten and understood. Choices that bring honor to the community and family are seen as moral. Making moral choices means living in a way that is honorable and honors the traditions of the culture. On the other hand, choices that bring dishonor or shame to the family or community are morally wrong. It is less about a written legal code and more about what brings honor to their relationships.

Along with the community focus, we also see a natural submission to the community's way of dealing with those moral wrongs. It is less important that an individual thinks if something is right; he/she wants to be convinced that the community that they are a part of will approve of their actions.

What happens if they violate the unwritten code of conduct? In a guilt/innocence culture, the community often waits for the law enforcement to pronounce guilt through ticketing, arrest, or prison. However, in an honor/shame culture, it is the group that determines the code of ethics and also enforces that code.

Enforcement in an honor/shame culture, to western eyes, seems harsh and often lacking compassion. Since honor has been violated, something must be done to restore the honor; usually this involves one of two options. With the first, honor is restored by publicly putting the offender to shame so that the community knows that it has been resolved. It is not enough for the offender to apologize or offer restitution. Often the currency that must be paid to restore honor is the currency of shame.

Consider the case of 'honor killings' which is a phenomenon precipitated by the need to restore honor. While it is the most extreme case of cultural action to restore honor, this action often goes unreported, and as a result it is impossible to know any real statistics. The United Nations estimated in 2010 that there were at least 5,000 such killings taking place every year, though the real number is probably much higher than what was reported. In fact, in a recent article published by The International Journal of Interdisciplinary and Multidisciplinary Studies, they estimate that the numbers of such killings reaches well into the 20,000 range worldwide.[15] Though this is often

---

[15] Sneha Singh, "Honour Killings in India: Need For a Composite and Strict Legal Framework," International Journal of Interdisciplinary and

seen as an Islamic practice when it occurs in the current worldwide climate, the cultural pressures that drive such behavior are no different than the pressures that existed in the days of Jesus Christ.

It is in the context of such an honor/shame culture that we must read and understand the Parable of the Prodigal Son. Our western eyes see a son that did wrong; their eyes would see a son that had caused shame. We are filled with delight when we read of the Father's forgiveness; they would have been angered at the Father's unwillingness to restore the family honor. Western culture misses how disrespectful the son's actions were to the family and community. In fact, we will have to work hard as we continue on our journey to understand the full meaning of our passage in light of the cultural context.

While we often interpret the Gospel message through the lense of our personal culture, it is best understood within the culture that it was given.

Multidisciplinary Studies (IJIMS), 2017, Vol 4, No.3, 279.

Chapter 5
Family Shame

Luke 15:11-12 11 And he said, A certain man had two sons: 12 And the younger of them said to his father, Father, give me the portion of goods that falleth to me. And he divided unto them his living.

The Son's Shame

Our parable begins with a very simple yet foundational statement. There was a man with two sons. Though the parable will seem to focus primarily on the younger son, Jesus wasn't telling this parable with only the younger son in mind. Over the years I have heard preachers make a point of this by calling this 'The Parable of the Prodigal Sons' (with their emphasis on the plural sons). I understand the desire to keep the older son in view; he is an important part of the narrative. However, Jesus basically tells us there was an older son who then drops out of the picture until the final scene of the story. In fact, to call both sons 'prodigal' actually changes the meaning of the text. Don't worry...we will get there eventually!

It is, however, very important throughout the narrative to keep the older son in mind. While we won't spend time yet fully uncovering all we know about him, it is with the 'older son' in the background that Jesus is giving this parable in the first place! Remember, it is the context of the Pharisees and their unwillingness to rejoice with Jesus over the redemption of sinners that forms the foundation for this detailed story. To dismiss the older brother as insignificant is to miss one of the most fundamental purposes of this parable: to uncover the heart of pharisaical thinking.

It is also significant that the conversation we are listening in on is taking place between the father and the younger son, who by cultural norms is the least worthy of the two to have a serious financial conversation. The position of the elder son was that of honor. It was the elder son that was responsible to keep the family intact after the father's death. Elder sons were to receive a double portion of the inheritance. The eldest son assumed a natural position of authority; when this was violated it created a deep cultural conflict.

Consider the story of Joseph and his brothers from Genesis 37. Though Joseph was only 17 years old when the story begins, we see Joseph being given the position of overseer by Jacob. We all know that Joseph was given a "coat of many colors." I won't dispute that the coat was colorful here in this book (though I have my doubts). Needless to say, the Hebrew wording in that passage says nothing of the color of the garment. Rather, he was given a long coat or the coat of an overseer. We also see Joseph lifted above his brethren through the vivid dreams. In each, Joseph was placed in the position of reverence, and the brothers made obeisance to him.

No wonder the brothers hated Joseph! Even if you think that Joseph was the 'favorite' son, their anger would have been stoked into fiery wrath primarily because he was one of the youngest sons and was being honored like one of the oldest sons. This was an outrage Joseph's brothers! This would have also been an outrage to the Pharisees to whom Jesus was talking. There were unwritten rules that guided their culture, and it took incredible nerve for the youngest son to even consider himself on the same plane as his father; this type of conversation was completely inappropriate. Their response, only one sentence into the parable, would have been, "Who does this boy think he is? He has no honor!"

Let's consider the younger son's request. "Father, give me the portion of goods that falleth to me." Give me! In the English that is a short sentence. In fact, there are many different ways that this interaction could be interpreted based on your understanding of English and sentence structure. Will you consider with me that there is a much deeper meaning in the words of the younger son: deeper and more disturbing.

In the Greek, the command to "give me" includes a few important 'road signs' to help us fully understand what was truly being communicated. Let's start simple; it is a verb. **Give**, didōmi (δίδωμι), is a request for action. The action that the son is communicating is for the father to 'give' or 'grant' to him something that he has no lawful right to possess. In fact, he has no right to make this request in the first place. Second, the verb is present tense. It wasn't a request for the future or a request for future consideration. **Give now**. Third, it is in second person. This clarifies the person that is the subject of the verb: you. He looked at his father and addressed him directly through his words. **You give now**. Fourth, it is imperative; the imperative tense makes this a clear command. Again, he isn't asking for his father to consider his request; he is making a demand on his father's good will. **I demand that you give now.** And of course there is an understood recipient to who will receive the action as well! **I demand that you give to me now.** This is much more that a simple request from a son…this is a demand that is bullish and downright disrespectful!

What was his demand? Though we might be tempted to view his demand as a grab for money or a desire for cash, the younger son's demands were as culturally charged as they were disrespectful. He demanded his portion of the family inheritance; this was scandalous and would have generated a great deal of angst toward this character in the parable.

The son's demand demonstrated a brassy disregard for the family inheritance. In western cultures, an inheritance is a luxury afforded by those that have amassed wealth or investments. The western inheritance is usually dispersed among the family through wills and estates and is primarily linked to the economic accomplishments of the previous generation. This was not the case for the inheritance of Bible times and for Jewish families. Consider these instructions given in regards to the family inheritance:

1. Every son received a portion with the eldest receiving a double portion. (Deuteronomy 21)
2. The inheritance was the family connection to the promised land. As a result, land was not to be disposed of permanently but was returned in the 'Year of Jubilee'. (Leviticus 25)
3. The inheritance was divided after the father had passed away. (Numbers 27)

The younger son's demand was in direct violation of the law of the land in regards to the inheritance and would have been viewed as barbaric in that culture. He demonstrated a shameful disregard for the purpose of the inheritance; it was intended to keep the sons connected to the land and prepare them for a life of success as the husband of a new family. His demand was selfish, shortsighted and shameful.

On a much deeper level, this demand was a blatant show of disrespect for his father as well. The laws regarding the inheritance were clear and well known: the inheritance was only to be distributed after the father had passed away. The son's demand for the inheritance was a clear cultural statement. What was he saying? "Dad, I wish you were dead!" Imagine the horror of hearing those words as a father today. They are sharp, biting, and communicate a level of hatred and animocity that would be difficult to surpass. The son was acting as if his father were already dead! When the younger son asked for the portion of his inheritance, he was showing a purposeful neglect for the cultural traditions as well as an offensive and vile disrespect toward his own father. The younger son had brought shame to the family.

Our final thought on the son's demand centers around a very simple and yet important truth about the Jewish inheritance. Though there might be some money involved, the inheritance was almost always tied directly to and centered around the family land. Land was much more than a commodity or investment; the land that the families lived on had been divided to them through the conquest of Canaan that we read about in the book of Joshua. The land was a direct connection to the promises of God and was worth more to the family than they could ever gain through selling it, but especially by selling any portion.

Because the land was given to the tribes by God, it was commanded that families never lose their connection to ownership. If a family fell on hard times and had to sell their land, they had the right to redeem it at a later date without fear of losing that connection. Included in the Old Testament Law was the provision that automatically returned that land back to the original family every 50 years, the Year of Jubilee. All of these provisions protected the family that owned the land, and rightly so; the land was a gift from God to be protected and preserved from generation to generation! For these reasons, liquidating land was not easy. The buyer would have to make the investment knowing that, in the end, it was not his land to keep, and he would eventually lose the rights of ownership. No matter how much had been poured into upkeep or upgrades, the land would eventually be deeded back to the original owners.

As a result, land sold for a fraction of what it was really worth. Selling land to convert into usable currency was an incredibly foolish act that would yield pennies on the dollar. That didn't matter to the younger son, though. Why? Because hearts that are set on rebellion and sin are blind to the foolishness of their choices. Sin deceives! When a heart is drawn toward temptation and yields to the brazen rebellion of the younger son, the consequences appear far away. Sin always delivers on the investment - a return of pain and heartache.

SALVATION IN FOCUS #1 - The Son

It is in these early stages of the book we will lay a foundation to understand the message of salvation within this parable. If we lay these early building blocks wrong, we will mis-interpret the entire parable. So, who does the younger son represent? Well, there are basically two options that scholars conclude. The first option is that he represents a wayward son in the sense of a believer that has strayed from fellowship with God the Father. We discussed this earlier in chapter two when we established the Scriptural context in which this parable is given. If this option is accurate, then the interpretation isn't dealing with salvation at all but rather a believer in the backslidden condition. Ask these questions to clarify. Were the Pharisees upset because Jesus fellowshipped with backslidden believers? Did Jesus come into the world to seek and to save the backslidden believer? Was there rejoicing in heaven over one backslidden believer that returned home? The answers are no, no, and no. The context of this parable clearly leads us to option number two.

The younger son represents unsaved humanity, once in fellowship with the Father but rebelling through a willful act of disobedience. Through Adam's sin, all of mankind was thrust into the grasp of the sin nature and are born apart from the fellowship of the 'Father.'

> **"Wherefore, as by one man sin entered into the world, and death by sin; and so death passed upon all men, for that all have sinned."**
> **-Romans 5:12**

We are all born in this sinful state. The younger son represents the separation and rebellion that characterizes the heart of unbelievers' hardened in their sin and living in defiance to the will of the Father. In essence, the act of rebellion that is seen in the opening lines of this parable happened thousands of years ago through the disobedience of Adam in the garden. Adam, given the choice to obey or rebel, chose the path that pleased his flesh and thereby plunged all of mankind into sinful bondage. It is in this state that each of us are born, apart from the father; we are already living in the 'far country', separate from the fellowship of the Father.

The Father's Shame

In honor/shame cultures the process of bringing about shame and restoring honor is a two way street. When someone acts in a way that brings shame to the family or community, there is a process of restoring honor to the family. First, there will be a denial of the actions. While Westerners would recognize this as lying to cover up the guilt, generally speaking, Eastern cultures would view lying as a justified and moral act to maintain the family honor. Remember, guilt comes not from doing wrong but from bringing shame on the family or community. If the deed can be denied or covered, then shame has been avoided, and life goes on.

If the shame cannot be denied or covered, it must be

avenged. It can be avenged through a payment of money, through an act of reciprocal shame, or through killing. The shame cannot be disregarded or ignored. That is the unwritten rule of honor/shame cultures and is so ingrained in their conscience that further shame is brought on a family that refuses to deal with their problems. Refusing to bring your rebellious son back under your authority is shameful itself! (For more information on the unwritten code of honor/shame cultures, visit www.honorshame.com)

In this culture, how should a father respond to a son that is demanding his inheritance before the father is dead? That is simple. A son of that nature would, at the very least, be disowned (dead to the family) and pushed out of the community; it is also quite possible that that son would be stoned to death to restore the family honor. Now before you decide that these two options are more extreme than the Biblical narrative would make provision for, consider the story of Stephen from Acts 7.

Stephen is introduced in Acts 6 and is described as a man "full of faith and the Holy Ghost…full of faith and power." He assisted the 12 disciples faithfully in the church through serving others and meeting spiritual needs. As the chapter progresses, Stephen's faith is transformed into powerful miracles and passionate preaching! It did not take long before his conspicuous ministry garnered the attention of the religious rulers of the synagogue. They arrested Stephen and brought him before the council; many of these men would have stood in judgment of Jesus Christ just a few years before. Their request? Stephen, tell us what you have been preaching.

This was a unique ministry opportunity for this young man. God was using him greatly in the community, and now he was being given an open floor with those that needed to hear the gospel the most...the unbelieving Jewish leaders! Knowing the rare opportunity he was being given, Stephen approached these men by appealing to the one thing that meant the most to them...their culture!

"The God of glory appeared unto our father Abraham, when he was in Mesopotamia, before he dwelt in Charran, And said unto him, Get thee out of thy country, and from thy kindred, and come into the land which I shall shew thee. Then came he out of the land of the Chaldaeans, and dwelt in Charran: and from thence, when his father was dead, he removed him into this land, wherein ye now dwell."

Stephen knew exactly what he was doing; he was drawing them in through the lure of their culture connection. There was an immediate connection to the cultural roots and Jewish heritage. He then progressed through a detailed history of the Jewish people: Joseph and his brothers, the Egyptian enslavement, the Great Exodus, Mount Sinai, the wilderness wanderings, and the special role that Moses played as a prophet to the people. He stops there in the narrative and makes a very clear point that though God spoke through Moses to the people, there were a group of Israelites that refused to submit to Moses and his words. They were resistant and hard-hearted; they were a rebellious people.

At this point, it is unclear what the members of the council would have been thinking. We see no response or interaction with them in the text...Stephen really hasn't said anything that they don't already know through their careful study of history and culture. And then Stephen took a deep breath and paused. He knew that the words he was about to speak would have consequences. The next few words that were migrating from his mind to his tongue were true words. There would be no disputing the accuracy of what he was getting ready to say. However, they were shameful words. Very shameful.

"Ye stiffnecked and uncircumcised in heart and ears, ye do always resist the Holy Ghost: as your fathers did, so do ye. Which of the prophets have not your fathers persecuted? and they have slain them which shewed before of the coming of the Just One; of whom ye have been now the betrayers and murderers: Who have received the law by the disposition of angels, and have not kept it."

Stephen held nothing back. He knew that his words would have consequences but what was said needed to be said. "Men of the council, in the same way that our Jewish forefathers rejected the prophet of God by rejecting Moses, you have rejected the very Son of God and have killed the innocent

Messiah! Though you may follow the outward circumcision, your heart is hard and is uncircumcised before Jehovah!" Stephen preached a message of shame. It triggered a cultural reaction in the hearts of the council. There was no hiding what Stephen had said...he had spoken in an open meeting with possibly hundreds looking on. There was only one option to bring honor back to the council. Stephen must be killed.

"When they heard these things, they were cut to the heart, and they gnashed on him with their teeth....Then they cried out with a loud voice, and stopped their ears, and ran upon him with one accord, And cast him out of the city, and stoned him."

The shame that was triggered by Stephen's words to the council was restored to honor as the men walked away from his lifeless body. In honor/shame cultures, shameful actions demand the restoration of honor. With that in mind, consider the actions of the father in our parable. Our first introduction to him comes in the form of these words:

"And he divided unto them his living."

The culture would demand that the father restore honor to the family through public shaming or disowning of the son. The family's name had been tarnished, and this demanded an open and harsh response to the son! Surprisingly, this did not happen. In fact, the first introduction to the father in this parable is his incredible act of grace and mercy. It is hard to communicate how unthinkable the father's reaction would have been to the Pharisees and the others listening. It cuts directly against the grain of the honor/shame dynamic in their culture.

There are three revealing truths that we see through the father's response to the rebellious son. First, the father's response was a response of grace. The essence of grace is this simple truth...unmerited favor. Grace is receiving something that is undeserved and unearned. The younger son had done nothing to receive the inheritance of the father! Though the inheritance was a normal family function in society, the son relinquished all 'right' to his inheritance the moment that he demanded it! It was only through indescribable grace that the father decided to divide his land and give the younger son his portion.

Secondly, the father demonstrates unbelievable mercy. At the very least, the son deserved to be shunned and expelled from the village. Quite often, actions like this resulted in sever beating or even death. The son had placed himself at the cultural mercy of the father, and the father extended wondrous mercy through his refusal to bring down such a harsh punishment. Mercy like that, however, is not without a price.

The third aspect of the father that is revealed in this simple introduction is his willingness to bear the shame of his rebellious son on himself. The honor/shame culture demands that shameful actions be confronted and that honor be restored. In short, it was just as shameful for the father to extend grace and mercy to the rebellious son as it was for the son to rebel in the first place! A father that refused to deal with a rebellious son was, in essence, bearing the shame on himself.

No doubt the Pharisees were bothered as they sat listening to Jesus speak. The son deserved to be punished yet the father was extending grace and mercy. It was a confusing introduction to the story because it cut across many of the cultural norms of the day. This, however, was only the beginning!

SALVATION IN FOCUS #2 - The Father

As we focus on salvation through this parable, we need to establish the identity of the father. The instinctive interpretation (because of the wording) is to assume that 'the father' represents God the Father. On a superficial reading, I don't think that there is much danger in making that assumption. However, when we dig deeper to understand the real meaning of the parable, the identity of the father becomes more important theologically.

The father's identity becomes evident through two textual hints: the Scriptural context within the passage as well as the actions of the father when he is introduced in the parable. First, the purpose of the parable is to reveal the heart condition of the Pharisees in response to Christ's actions. Think back to the contextual introduction that we uncovered. The issue at hand was simple...the Pharisees were angered that Jesus was eating and fellowshipping with sinners. Jesus is at the center of the controversy, so it would make sense that Jesus is at the center of the parable to reveal the reality of their own rebellion. Secondly, within the context of the passage, it was the fact that Jesus was extending grace and mercy to sinners that unwrapped their inner rebellion. In the parable, the father's first actions are to extend grace and mercy to the undeserving son. Notice how the father and Jesus are one and the same.

The greatest evidence, however, that the father is best represented by Jesus Christ is this fact: it was Jesus Christ that bore the shame and guilt of my rebellion through his offer of grace and mercy! In the same way that the father in the parable chose to take the shame of the son on himself, it was Jesus that bore the cross of my shame! It is through Jesus's name that unmerited favor and reconciliation is offered to all mankind!

Before we can fully appreciate the wondrous nature of the Father's mercy, however, we need to fully understand the depths of our sin. It is with this in mind that Jesus moves into the next portion of His parable...the shameful living of the younger son.

Chapter 6
Riotous Living

13 And not many days after the younger son gathered all together, and took his journey into a far country, and there wasted his substance with riotous living. 14 And when he had spent all, there arose a mighty famine in that land; and he began to be in want.

It didn't take long for the son to put his plans into action. He was fed up with all the trappings of the Jewish culture and Jewish life. He took full advantage of his father's gracious actions, and within a few short days he was gone. He fled to a far country and lived a life of excess and waste off the goodness of his father. If the Pharisees hated the younger son already, this would have driven them mad! Before the rebellious son could make his escape, though, he faced an obstacle that is not clear within the text but would have been very clear to the listeners.

While the father did graciously give the son his portion of the inheritance, it was most likely not in cash or currency, but in the form of land. Remember, the land was the promise given to Abraham, and it was the land that was divided to the Israelite tribes as they entered and conquered Canaan. This presented a real problem for the young man. While land does have value, selling the land inheritance created three huge hurdles he had to overcome.

First, land is not spendable currency! While land is valuable and under normal circumstances would probably have fetched a nice price, the young man was able to resolve this issue in a matter of days. He had to sell the land (liquidate the assets) in order to have money to take with him on his adventure! So the first hurdle is the fact that he must sell the land to get the money. The second hurdle would have been very apparent to the listeners that day. Selling family land was almost unheard of because it was not permanent. While there were a few exceptions (almost all had to do with the land remaining in the family), every 50 years land that had been sold was to put back into the name of the family that had originally received it during the conquest of Canaan. In other words, a person that bought land knew that it really wasn't his land but would be given back after a period of time.

The third hurdle was probably the biggest of the three. Under the circumstances of the son's rebellion, no respectable Jewish person would ever think of even purchasing the land! The younger son was acting in shame, and it would only bring further shame to others if they involved themselves in his scandalous behavior by purchasing the inherited land. The fact that he was willing to part with Jehovah's promised land was unthinkable. Maybe you remember the story from I Kings where Ahab went on a walk and saw Naboth's vineyard. Ahab, the King of Israel, approached Naboth and asked if he could have the land. Naboth's response demonstrates the intense relationship that the Jewish people had with their land inheritance.

I Kings 21: 3 And Naboth said to Ahab, The LORD forbid it me, that I should give the inheritance of my fathers unto thee.

Naboth refused to give his land to the king and ultimately lost his life protecting the inheritance that had been passed down from his fathers. The inherited land was sacred! No respectable Jew would ever agree to purchase land that was tainted by the son's shame.

These three issues would make the selling of the land very difficult. However, we see he sold it very quickly. Within a few days he was off on his escapade with cash in hand….probably having sold the land for far less than what it was really worth in order to liquidate it so quickly. A modern version of this story would have the younger son taking the title to his father's vehicle in to a "Title Loan" lender and receiving pennies on the dollar for the actual value of the vehicle. It is possible to liquidate land quickly, but you have to settle for a fraction of what it is actually worth.

There are two incredible life lessons that are demonstrated in the son's behavior. First, people that are consumed with sin will do foolish and illogical things to satisfy their own lusts. There is no thought for how their actions will cost them dearly in the long run or how they are settling for a future that will be filled with disappointment and heartache. The younger son was literally trading his future away for a fool's pittance. Second, a person that is the attendant to sin holds nothing back; they are all in. The son gathered 'all' of his belongings as he prepared for his journey. He had no plans on returning to the father. He was headed to a far country.

...and took his journey into a far country...

Jesus was speaking in a Jewish context to a Jewish audience. There was no doubt in their minds that the 'far country' was referring to a Gentile land where the young man could leave his cultural and religous heritage behind. He had turned his back on his father, and now he was turning his back on his own people. This was repulsive to the Jewish listeners. The very community that had raised and supported him through his early years was now the object of his scorn.

It is very obvious that the boy had put very little thought into his journey. He had no idea what he was getting into or what to expect when he got there. He had set his eyes on pleasure, and nothing short of that goal would satisfy. Often when we see a person making the move toward sin, we assume that it will be a slow movement away from the father. The younger son demonstrates to us that when sinful man sets his heart toward sin, it isn't always a slow progression. Our sinful flesh can take us into a far country very quickly; separate from the father and far away from the benefits of sonship.

...and there wasted his substance with riotous living.

Have you ever wondered why this parable is called *The Parable of the Prodigal Son*? My guess is that you probably think that *prodigal* means wayward or rebellious. How often have you heard a despondent parent speak of their own 'prodigal' child? I have heard it often enough that I know people don't know what *prodigal* means! Don't look it up quite yet. It will make more sense as we uncover the truths within this part of the parable.

So we read that the younger son wasted away all of his posessions. The word *wasted* is perfectly acceptable as a translation, but it is only acceptable if we really understand the foundation that it is built on. It comes from a Greek word (διασκορπίζω diaskorpizo) which means "to winnow away" or "to squander." Winnowing is the process of taking harvested grains and separating the usable part from the chaff. In Bible days, this was done by taking the pile of harvested grain and throwing it up into the air; the chaff would blow away and the usable grain would fall back to the floor. As you repeated this over and over, eventually there was no chaff left in the pile. It had all been winnowed away.

Imagine a young man that is experiencing life to the fullest for the first time. He is free from the shackles of parents and the cares of a watching community. He is free to spend his money however he wants, on whatever he wants, whenever he wants! It is as if he is taking piles of cash and throwing them into the air, and the wind gently carries it away, never to be seen. In a literal sense, that money has been winnowed away through wasteful spending. This is the picture that Jesus is wanting us to see as he describes the actions of the rebellious son. Yet it isn't his rebellion that earns him the title 'The Prodigal Son.' It is his wasteful and extravagent spending! *Prodigal* doesn't mean rebellious or defiant at all; it means overflowing in abundance, unsparing, and liberal. It is the son's extravagant and lavish lifestyle that earns him the title of "The Prodigal."

In a sense, there are two people in this story that qualify as 'prodigal' in their behavior. Though we would shudder to call the father prodigal, we will see that he lives up to that name as well! I would ask that you tuck that thought away, though. We will cover the father's lavish grace in a later chapter.

Sinful people driven by sinful desires make sinful choices. The young son is no different. We see that he squanders his money away on 'riotous living' and excess. He sells the family land for pennies on the dollar and then goes and wastes it all! It is as if he has no consciousness of his father's sacrifice and the value that the land had to his future. The passage doesn't go into much more detail in regards to the sinful lifestyle. There is, however, an interesting comment made by the older brother later in the story. In verse 30, during the interaction between the father and the older son, he makes a statement about his brother's actions. "But as soon as this thy son was come, which hath devoured thy living with harlots..." The older brother makes a claim of sexual impropriety along with other issues that are obvious in the story. The bottom line is this; can we trust the older brother? Is he stating something that is true, or is he attempting to denegrate his brother even more in order to make himself look better?

While it is completely possible, and maybe even likely, that the younger brother was involved in immoral behavior with prostitutes, that was not Jesus's point. In fact, whether or not he paid for sexual relations is such an incredibly small part of the story and insignifigant to the shame culture that was judging him. Rather, Jesus is revealing the heart attitude of the Pharisees who were more concerned about the sins of others than the sins of their own hearts. Their selfish heart was revealed through the older brother that was more concerned about pointing out the sins of his younger sibling than rejoicing that he had returned home.

14 And when he had spent all, there arose a mighty famine in that land; and he began to be in want.

Welcome to the daily dose of reality. If you live fast and loose it will catch up with you sooner or later! I have heard this saying many times in my life and so it is not original to me. "You can choose your sins, but you can't choose your consequences." This has never been as true as it was in the younger son's life. He winnowed away his money in riotous and sinful living. He made friends, bought influence, and wasted all of the inheritance on the temporary cares of this world.

As we consider the depths of the son's despair, I want us to see first that this was a predictable outcome for the younger son. When you choose to live life seeking after the flesh, the inevitable outcome is pain and suffering. Galatians 6:7-8 describes it this way. "Be not deceived; God is not mocked: for whatsoever a man soweth, that shall he also reap. For he that soweth to his flesh shall of the flesh reap corruption; but he that soweth to the Spirit shall of the Spirit reap life everlasting." Paul begins this simple truth with these words - "Be not deceived." Don't be deceived! God will not be made a mockery. No one has ever beat the system, and no one ever will. When you sow to the flesh, you will reap destruction. It is that simple and is plainly unavoidable! You cannot sow to the desires of the flesh and then expect to reap the harvest of righteous living. It doesn't happen. It has never happened. It never will happen.

When Adam was given a simple command of "Do not eat" in the garden, the choice to obey was as simple as it gets. Obey and be blessed; disobey and die. There was no getting around the consequence of the sin - spiritual death. Adam did not die physically that day, and even after he had sinned, he still had the ability to talk to God and understand the reality of his sin. Adam's death and the prodigal's death are one and the same. They are both removed from fellowship with the father and are distant with no right to being restored.

Sadly, we see the predictabilty of sin played out in the lives of people all around us, do we not? People will live to satisfy the longings of the flesh and sin and then are surprised when the consequences are painful and difficult. Hear this and hear it well. Life is always better when we live it God's way. Obedience always brings blessing, and disobedience always brings hurt. The prodigal son learned this through his experiences; the outcome of his rebellion was predictable.

Secondly, whatever the son thought he would find in his travels, he did not find! No one travels to the far country looking for heartache. People don't seek out sin for its consequences but for its pleasures. As is recorded in Hebrews 11, there is "pleasure of sin for a season" and it is this pleasure that the sinful flesh is longing after. The pleasure is fleeting, though. Soon the season of fun is over, and the reality of consequences hit home....and the consequences of sin are harsh and devastating. Verse 14 ends with this phrase, "and he began to be in want." The prodigal was looking for pleasure but instead he found pain. He sought after the things that would satisfy the flesh. I'm sure he was satisfied for a short while but as with all sin, there are consequences that will eventually catch up with you.

It is interesting that our Lord uses the occurance of famine in this parable. Remember, He is not giving a historical narrative but is crafting a story that will accomplish the purpose of revealing the heart sins of the Pharisees. Christ could have used a variety of natural disasters to communicate the helplessness of the younger son - flood, mighty storm, sever illness, or even an earthquake. Each of these could have been crafted into the story in some way to communicate the son's desperate state, but Jesus chose to use a famine. We must ask the question...Why a famine?

It is no mistake that Jesus used a famine. As we have often done in previous chapters, we must put ourselves in the culture of the day to really grasp the seriousness of the situation. While famines are relatively unheard of in our Western culture, they are a worldwide reality and would have been so in Jesus's day. In fact, famines are found often in the Scriptures, especially in the Old Testament. In Genesis 12 Abraham and Sarai experienced a famine that drove them to the fertile land of Egypt. Genesis 26 records the famine that Isaac experienced. Joseph and his brothers experienced a famine that drove the brothers to Egypt to buy grain; God used this to reconnect Joseph with them and establish his rule over them. We find famines in Ruth, II Samuel, I and II Kings, Nehemiah, as well as Luke and Acts.

Famines serve as more than just reminders of the fragility of creation; they represent the hand of God in judging people. The Old Testament Scriptures are clear...God's powerful hand is evident through famines. Psalm 105:16 states that God calls for famine upon the land. Isaiah 51 even describes famine as one of God's tools to bring judgment on His enemies. (II Samuel 24, Jeremiah 15, Ezekiel 5 all reinforce this idea) Famines are such a unique event because they can be brought on by so many different events that are unconnected yet come together to create a severe food shortage. For the religous in Christ's culture, the hand of Jehovah is seen through the occurence of famine.

Famines also create desperate need in the land. Our Westernized view of food availability keeps us from really grasping the seriousness of a crippling food shortage. We are so far removed from the production of our food (maybe with the exception of rural communities) that it would not even take a shortage of food to create a modern famine. Any serious disruptions in the financial system, the transportation network, or the power grid would bring food distribution to a halt, and millions of people in urban settings would find themselves without food in a matter of days. Chaos would ensue! In fact, this is the exact storyline for countless novels and movies because it plays on our greatest fear...the confusion and disorder that comes from having no food or water. With all this in mind, a famine was a fitting circumstance to arise in this parable. It represented the hand of God working in the affairs of men, specifically bringing judgement to the young son. In fact, the Pharisees would think it to be completely reasonable that God would judge a son that had acted so shamefully toward his father and his community. Simply put, the son deserved every ounce of the punishment he was receiving. This part of the parable would have pleased the Pharisees. The rebellious son was finally being brought to his knees!

SALVATION IN FOCUS #3 - Apart from the Father

Consider with me how the son's position in the far away land represents the distance between sinful mankind and the Savior. No matter how good we may think we are, Scripture is clear that we are all born in sin!

- *Psalms 51:5 - Behold, I was shapen in iniquity; and in sin did my mother conceive me.*
- *Psalms 58:3 - The wicked are estranged from the womb: they go astray as soon as they be born, speaking lies.*
- *Romans 5:12 - Wherefore, as by one man sin entered into the world, and death by sin; and so death passed upon all men, for that all have sinned:*

- *Romans 3:10 - As it is written, There is none righteous, no, not one:*
- *1 John 1:10 - If we say that we have not sinned, we make him a liar, and his word is not in us.*

People often struggle with their interpretation of this parable because they don't understand that for each individual, born in sin, our story begins in the 'far country.' There is no going there on life's journey or choosing to live in rebellion to the 'father' that brings that separation. It is there from birth! Adam's disobedience drove a wedge between mankind and the Creator that exists from the very beginning in our hearts. Every person is born apart from God, living for self, and seeking to fulfill the desires of the flesh. No one is born in fellowship with the father, regardless of family background or upbringing.

Sinful man also stands in the place of God's judgement. As the famine represents God's hand of wrath on the young son, the sinful separation that exists in our heart places us squarely as a target of God's eternal wrath and punishment. As the son's actions have brought shame, every man is born in shame and in need of spiritual reconciliation that only the 'father' can give. Only the father in our parable can actually restore the sonship now that the fellowship has been broken.

Chapter 7
Feeding the Swine

v.15 And he went and joined himself to a citizen of that country; and he sent him into his fields to feed swine.

Our previous chapter ended with the prodigal son suffering through the wrath of a famine with nothing left of his inheritance. He had spent all, had nothing to his name, and all his 'new friends' had forsaken him! And yet with his circumstances turning hopeless, he refused to go home. I think we often gloss over the signifigance of verse 15 as it relates to the attitude of the prodigal son; we would think that at this point in the story, he would make the turn toward home. Yet he doesn't. Instead he puts together a scheme that he thinks will get him out of his predicament. Helpless. Homeless. Penniless. He refuses to humble himself and go home; he has his own plan.

Why didn't he just go home? Going home was the last thing

this young man wanted to do! To go home was to admit failure and face the wrath of the father. He would be owning the shame he had caused the family. He would have to face the disapproval of the community and bear the humiliation of the entire village. No. Going home was to admit failure; this young man wasn't ready to admit his own sinfulness yet.

What was his brilliant plan? It seemed simple enough in his mind and under normal circumstances might have provided him with enough income to make ends meet. His bright idea - let me find someone in town who needs some part time work done, and I can make back enough money to survive. The Merriam Webster Dictionary defines delusion as "a persistent false belief that is maintained despite the indisputable evidence to the contrary." This young man was living in a delusion if he thought that he would find work during a time of famine. He refused to see how hopeless the situation was and decided to press onward with his foolish plan.

"He joined himself to a citizen of that country." He found a person of means. Though there was a famine in the land, there were still people of substance that had money and influence. In fact, as this part of the story progresses, we see that this person also owned pigs and possibly other livestock. The prodigal son recognized that he needed to find a person of influence that could help him; a person with enough means to offer food and payment so that he could earn back some of the money he had lost. In his mind this was the only way to make things right and set his life back in order.

Isn't it funny how we can be blinded by wrong choices? The younger son is going down a path of destruction and can't even see that there are major problems with his plan. First, there was a famine in the land. Though a person of means would still have food and finances to offer, there were probably many people that were begging for food and work. The job he hoped for, that would save his skin, simply didn't materialize. The second issue was with his nationality - he was Jewish and a foreigner. He was the one that had travelled away from his Jewish culture and home country, and now he was the stranger in the land. He wasn't a local boy looking for work; he was a beggar taking work from those that lived there. Third, his undisciplined lifestyle would make him a poor choice for almost any type of work. He had proven himself to be disobedient, disrespectful, unthoughtful, wasteful, and prideful. Is this the type of person you would want to hire to do work around your home or business? I think not - this is the type of person you want to keep as far away as possible! Interestingly, he did end up with work; he had no idea, though, what he was in for as a young Jewish boy.

There is an interesting dynamic that happens between the citizen that gave him work (if you can call it that) and our prodigal son. The Greek word for 'joined' (κόλλα, kolla) is unique and very descriptive. It literally means that he 'glued' himself. It might be easy to think that the young man happened to find a generous soul that decided to help him out, but in reality this outcast beggar found a person that had means, and he attached himself. In today's language we would call him a leech. A parasite. A freeloader. He found a person that he thought could help him out and then 'glued' himself so as to get what he wanted.

I remember in my first summer as a youth pastor we travelled to Nova Scotia, Canada and visited a Christian camp. It was a 'missions trip' that was focused on helping the camp staff prepare for a busy summer of camp. One evening, after a long day of scraping and painting, we all headed down to the coolness of the creek to refresh our bodies. It was enlivening! The cool clear water was stimulating to the senses, and for a few moments we were lost in the tranquility of natures's beauty. That is until one of the girls yelled, at the top of her lungs I might add, "Leech!" As we all scrambled out of the water it became evident that we were not the only living things enjoying that cool creek water that evening! I can't say that it was horrific or gruesome (only two teens ended up with a leech on them) but I can say that the few leeches that did happen to attach onto legs were quickly removed. In frantic manner the teens wanted those blood-suckers off of their legs right now!

What do you do when a leech (a poor beggar boy that has wasted all of his money) attaches himself to you and is only trying to use you? You send him away to feed the swine! When he sent him away it wasn't to feed the pigs out at the barn. There were no barns in ancient Palestine. Our modern American understanding of farm life has given us a grave misunderstanding of the events that are happening in this verse.

Pigs often free-roamed in the public land beyond the town borders. It would be similar to how cattle were allowed to roam freely in the early American western lands, knowing that they were owned by someone and would eventually be claimed. Swine were a free-ranging animal in this culture; going out to feed the swine meant leaving the town and heading into the surrounding land. When the citizen wanted to get rid of the leech on his leg, he flicked him off and sent him to feed the swine. This was no act of kindness. He was getting rid of a problem. Nothing in the text ever hints that the 'kind' citizen was acting out of compassion as he sent him out to feed the pigs; rather, he sent him far away to feed the pigs!

This also created a incredible friction in the minds of the Pharisees; good Jews avoided anything to do with pigs! The very thought of a Jewish man being reduced to the level of feeding swine was repulsive and repugnant! It was established through the law of Moses that pigs were among the ceremonially unclean animals and had become ingrained in the minds and culture of the Jews. From a practical perspective, pigs are physically filthy as well! Even if you removed the religous angle, the thought of being a pig farmer automatically suggests images of filth and squalor.

16 And he would fain have filled his belly with the husks that the swine did eat: and no man gave unto him.

There is one more cultural aspect that is often overlooked and misunderstood. "He would have filled his belly with the husks…" As gross as this sounds, we often conjur up imagery of the prodigal son desiring to 'belly up' to the pig trough and eat the slop that the farmer had put out for them to eat. Remember, though, there is no barn, no trough, and consequently there was no 'slop' for the pigs. I realize that it makes for an easy comparison to compare his condition to that of a hired hand on a pig farm, but the reality is that his condition was much worse and far more dire. If you remember from the previous pages, swine were often let loose into the wilderness to wander around eat whatever forage they could find. This was occuring during a famine…whatever edible food/forage was available for humans had long been picked or gathered people. So as the young man, our prodigal son, wandered along with the swine, he watched as they ate the only thing available for them - Karob pods. (Also spelled carob)

The karob pod, sometimes called a 'locust bean', is a small shrub in the bean family that bears long fibrous pods. While there are edible varieties today and man has created ingeneous ways to harvest the nutritional content of the pods, no such processes were used in this era. The karob pod was worthless in regards to human consumption and was practically indigestible. Imagine sitting down to eat dinner and the waitress brings out a nice big plate of old dried okra pods. Though they are not related in any way, and I am not suggesting they are the same, tough and fibrous okra pods give a relatively good comparison to what a karob pod would provide in nutritional value. They are tough to chew, hard to swallow, nutritionally empty, and practically impossible for human digestion.

Guess what…pigs love karob pods! They may be a little tough to chew, but they have the complex digestive tract needed to break down the complex cellulose into usable energy. While they might prefer something a little more tasty, there was nothing holding them back that day from rooting around under the shrubs and filling their belly with the husks that were abundant on the ground! It didn't take long for the young man to see what was happening; the pigs were eating to their heart's content and yet he had no one willing to even give him food to eat. The pigs were full, but he was hungry.

Before we move on, let's define a very important term: rock bottom. No doubt you have heard these words - "That person finally hit rock bottom." What does that mean? It is really simple. It describes a person that has chosen a path that has led to destruction and pain. Rock bottom describes a person that has come to the end of their path and has realized that they made a wrong turn somewhere in the past. People at rock bottom become desperate; it is often at this point that real change can take place because people recognize their hopeless condition. People hit rock bottom for many reasons: drugs, alcohol, overwhelming debt, addictions…or for taking your portion of the family inheritance and wasting it on riotous living. It is at this point that the prodigal son has hit rock bottom!

As we come to the end of this first section of the parable, consider what our Savior has done through His teaching so far. Jesus uses His skill as a master teacher to begin shaping the story in a way that creates a specific response with the Pharisees. In fact, Jesus has described the younger son in such a way that would have infuriated the Pharisees and sharpened their anger toward the son. He disrespected his father, disregarded his culture, wasted the family inheritance, had his fill of riotous and immoral living, begged for food, and ended up wishing he could lower himself to the ground and eat with the pigs. His character was sealed in the minds of the Pharisees. They absolutely hated the younger son!

SALVATION IN FOCUS #4 - Not of Works

Ever since spiritual fellowship was broken through Adam's sin, mankind has looked for ways to restore fellowship with God. Consider the interaction that happened just a few short years after Adam was expelled from the Garden. Cain and Abel were both given the opportunity to sacrifice to God; they both brought their offering and presented it in worship. Abel obeyed and brought the sacrifice of the flock. His sacrifice was accepted by God because he chose God's path. Cain, on the other hand, chose to come to

God through his own works and presented the fruit of the ground. This was a sacrifice that was logical to him and was his attempt to approach God in his own way.

The prodigal son also had his own plan. When he realized the desperation of his condition, he tried to come up with his own solution…and it failed miserably. It was only then that he reached the end of his rope and came to himself. He realized that there was only one way to make things right, and it involved humility, repentance, confession. The path of a sinner is equally as hard. Spiritual separation from the Father has placed us in a position of hunger, want, and great need.

This is exactly where mankind stands in sin. We are separate from the Father with no way to restore the fellowship. Men desperately try to work their way to God and fail; however, the best attempts at righteousness stand as filth before a righteous and holy God. It is only when a person realizes the depths to which his sin has taken him that he has hit 'rock bottom' and is ready to come to Jesus by faith alone!

Chapter 8
I Will Arise

17 And when he came to himself, he said, How many hired servants of my father's have bread enough and to spare, and I perish with hunger! 18 I will arise and go to my father...

As we move into the middle part of this parable we need to put ourselves back into the minds of the Pharisees that were listening to Jesus. He had just described the shocking actions of a rebellious son and all of his depraved behavior. Christ had detailed the son's defiance of the cultural norms, the wasteful spending, and the improper behavior that brought him to poverty and begging. In the mind of the Pharisees, the story could have ended with the boy wishing to eat with the pigs. That is what he deserved.

In a guilt/shame culture there is little room for forgiveness. If a son has brought shame to the family, that shame must be settled. The concept of a father offering forgiveness or a son asking for forgiveness in these situations was beyond the norms of their culture. In fact, we see this in the Luke passage, though we often miss the signifigance of the language: "I am no more worthy to be called thy son." "This my son was dead." The son's actions had produced an unresolvable tension that had played itself out many times in their culture. There was to be no resolution. The son was dead to the father.

This cultural concept continues to play into the picture that is being created of the Pharisees and their ungracious spirit. There was nothing in their religious system that would allow for forgivness and grace to the undeserving. Apart from the works of righteousness and obedience to the law, undeserving sinners had no standing with the Heavenly Father and did not deserve His mercy. To the Pharisees, the son's rock bottom moment should have been the end of the story. Period. Thankfully, it was at the rock bottom moment that the young son recognized two things: his inability to save himself and his father's power to deliver him from his condition.

I want us to consider a concept in verse 17 that can cause confusion in a discussion about salvation, but is very clearly stated within this narrative. The uncertainty is centered around a simple phrase in verse 17, "when he came to himself." In what regards did the prodigal son/sinner come to himself? What does it mean for a sinner to come to the realization that he is in sin and that his only hope is the father? The description given by our Lord is both clear and precise. The son, who was in the position of being dead to the father, was able to recognize his deadness. How is this possible, if the son was dead? Isn't it impossible for a dead person to think or know? Wouldn't a person that is spiritually dead be "totally unable" to even recognize his own sinfulness?

At the center of this issue is this question: "Is sinful man able to recognize his sinfulness?" Thankfully this passage defines for us the extent of what our deadness to the father means in regards to our salvation. In regards to our sinful state, the total depravity of man is seen through the description of the rebellious son. He rejected the goodness of the father and was living in the depths of his sin; there was no regard to the religious, ethical, or moral boundaries that he crossed as he travelled to the far country. Yet, even in the depths of that depravity, he came to himself. There are two things that this verse reveals are necessary for the "coming to yourself" moment in the life of an unbeliever.

One, it requires understanding the depths of your own sin. Since God has placed in all of mankind the conscience of good and evil (Genesis 3, Romans 1), it isn't difficult to recognize that man can perceive his own sinfulness. Have you ever talked to an alcoholic that is drunk, a drug addict that is strung out, or a man addicted to pornography? In that discussion, there is often a recognition of the depths to which they have fallen. Years ago, I specifically remember talking to a man that was absolutely dominated by alcohol. He cried on my shoulder and bemoaned the depths that his alcohol had taken his mind and body. There was no missing the fact that he was caught in his sin, and he freely admitted it. Day after day he recognized that alcohol was controlling his life, and he was 'feeding the swine' with his life. To say that a sinner is unable to recognize the sinfulness of his condition clearly contradicts the letter as well as spirit of this passage.

Along with this truth comes a seeming paradox contained within the Scriptures. As we interpret the son's journey and apply it to our own journey toward redemption, it would seem that the son is acting alone and independent of the father. In other words, it seems as though he is coming to his father on his own terms which puts the emphasis of his 'salvation experience' on man's actions as opposed to God's grace and mercy. Is this really the case? Consider these thoughts. First, the son has proven that he is helpless to save himself. The son has demonstrated that his lifestyle is corrupt and vile with no hint of goodness. The son has driven a wedge between the father and himself that cannot be resolved by any actions of his own. There is nothing left for him to do but turn to the father and beg for his mercy.

Second, the son demonstrates a complete dependence on his father for grace and mercy. There is no heart pride in the son's return. His heart's cry is overwhelmingly clear that he knows he can do nothing to help himself, and his father is the only one that has the resources. Third, to say that the son's turn toward home equates to any type of meritorious work overlooks the clear teaching from this passage. Often we will hear it stated that if man has any part in salvation then it is not all of God. This insinuates that somehow our turning to God in faith is a work that dimishes from the grace and mercy of the Savior. A necessary step must then be added into the salvation process; God must bring life to the unregenerate soul before that person can come to Him. Is that what we see here? Clearly not. To say that the son's act of turning toward home represents anything but faith dimishes the glory of the father's mercy!

> *Ephesians 2:8-9 "For by grace are ye saved through faith; and that not of yourselves: it is the gift of God: Not of works, lest any man should boast."*

Not only does the "coming to yourself" moment require an understanding of our sin, it demands a realistic view of the father's goodness! It wasn't just a recognition of his sin that would put the son on the repentance road; it was the knowledge that there was someone that was able to meet his need! "How many hired servants of my father's have bread enough and to spare, and I perish with hunger!" The prodigal son recognized that all he needed was already provided by the father for those under his care. There was no earning the father's mercy. There was no deserving the father's mercy. The son could only make the turn toward home and place himself under the mercy of the father. There is a wonderful peace in knowing that salvation is not of our own merits but rather by the effectual work of Jesus Christ on the cross. As the hymn states, "nothing in my hand I bring, simply to thy cross I cling! God, I am unable, but you are able! This is the bad news/ good news of salvation. I am a sinner and unable to save myself, and yet there is one greater than I that has more than enough to provide for my needs! Amen!

Another very important aspect of the son's turn toward home is assumed in the passage but cannot be assumed in man's salvation. There must be a knowledge of the goodness of the father! The son's turn toward home was facilitated by two truths: I can't do for myself, and there is one that can! He knew of his father's resources, and he knew that he freely gave them to those who were his servants. The son glanced toward home and longed for the good grace of the father. With that in mind, can man be saved apart from a knowledge of the grace of God? We are talking about a very specific grace that God has shown mankind....the unmerited favor accessible to man through Christ's sacrifice on the cross.

> *Romans 5:8-10 8 But God commendeth his love toward us, in that, while we were yet sinners, Christ died for us. 9 Much more then, being now justified by his blood, we shall be saved from wrath through him. 10 For if, when we were enemies, we were reconciled to God by the death of his Son, much more, being reconciled, we shall be saved by his life.*

Is it possible for a man to be reconciled to God apart from the knowledge of Jesus Christ? In the same way that the son only knew to turn in faith toward the father becaue he knew of his goodness, man can only come to God through knowledge of the goodness of Jesus Christ. I am reminded of Romans 10:14 which states, "How then shall they call on him in whom they have not believed? and how shall they believe in him of whom they have not heard? and how shall they hear without a preacher?" Notice how the emphasis is placed on the believing as a result of the hearing! We see this pattern all throughout the gospels as the followers of Christ begin sharing their faith with others; it is a pattern that is seen clearly in the testimony of Phillip and the Ethiopian's conversion.

It is in Acts 8 that we read of the interaction between Phillip and this man. I remember hearing this passage preached numerous times as a young child. My parents are missionaries, and as many missionaries do, we travelled on deputation for a little over two years. During that time I heard my dad preach week after week, and inevitably, he landed on the same sermon on numerous occasions. Acts 8 seemed to be a favorite as he preached a sermon titled "3 Men on the Road to Gaza." The first man is the Ethiopian; he is sitting in his chariot with the Scriptures opened to Isaiah. Phillip sees him reading and confused, so he asks him if he understands what he is reading? Of course, the answer is no. " How can I, except some man should guide me?" His plea is simple; I don't know what I am reading unless some man (which turns out is Phillip) guides me through the Scriptures. At this point, the Ethiopian is lost, confused and completely unaware of the wonderful grace that is offered to him through Jesus Christ.

It is at this point that our point is made. They begin reading. "He was led as a sheep to the slaughter; and like a lamb dumb before his shearer, so opened he not his mouth." The man turned to Phillip and asked a simple question: "Of whom speaketh the prophet this? of himself, or of some other man?" We see the third man introduced at this point in the story. I can still see the excitement on my dad's face when he would get to this part of the sermon; Philip opened his mouth "...and preached unto him Jesus!" You see, there is no gospel without Jesus! A sinner will remain lost in his sin until he knows about the gracious and merciful work of Jesus Christ on the cross of Calvary. As sinners born in sin, there has to be a point where we are introduced to Jesus, just as this unsaved Ethiopian was that day.

In our parable, we see the same truth played out in the younger son. It was the knowledge of the father's love that brought clarity to his thinking and pointed him toward home. The son came to himself and recognized two things: his own sin and the love of the father.

SALVATION IN FOCUS #5 - What is the Gospel

I think too often we make the gospel more intricate than Scripture does. We begin adding layers of complexity while at the same time insisting that the sinner understand all sorts of foundational doctrinal truths: creation, the Trinity, inspiration, the rapture just to name a few. While all these are important and should be studied and sought after by the student of the Scriptures, nowhere in Scripture do we see the gospel made complex. In fact, we see just the opposite. The gospel is very simple. In John 4 we see one such instance played out through the interaction between Jesus and the woman that met him at the well. The gospel was made plain; there is bad news (we are sinners) and good news (Christ offers forgiveness). Have you ever considered why that woman, after receiving the good news of Christ's mercy, was able to become a witness so quickly? In that passage, she immediately goes into the local village and begins proclaiming the gospel to her friends and family, and a multitude of them come to know Christ. How could she transition between sinner and evangelist in a matter of a few verses? Because the gospel is simple!

In I Corinthians 15, Paul clearly describes the gospel: Christ died for our sins, was buried, rose again the third day, and was seen of many. There really are only two working parts to his explanation of the gospel. First, we are sinners; second, Christ died, was buried, and rose again. Paul proclaims the bad news/good news of the gospel which is the same bad news/good news that Jesus communicated to the woman at the well. This is exactly what we see played out in our parable as well, which is our Savior's clear explanation of the gospel. The son knew the desperation of his own condition (bad news) and turned his heart toward the goodness of the father (good news). That is the simplicity of the gospel.

---

18 I will arise and go to my father, and will say unto him, Father, I have sinned against heaven, and before thee, 19 And am no more worthy to be called thy son: make me as one of thy hired

servants.

Among the issues surrounding salvation that can cause confusion and disagreement is the discussion involving the 'sinner's prayer.' I was first introduced to this issue when I was in upper elementary school. We moved to a new city and immediately began looking for a church to call our home. Over time, our family settled in to a local church that had an incredible outreach/evangelism program that was the clear focus of the entire ministry; it quickly became the focus of our family also as the family faithfully attended weekly 'soul winning' and as I personally did my best to never miss out on teen visitation. Over time, though, I began noticing something different with my parents. The excitement that had surrounded our first few years in the church faded quickly. I could tell that there was some issue that was stealing their joy. Sadly, the day came when we attended our final service. That evening, may parents sat down with me and my two sisters and explained the issue.

The issue was 'easy believism.' A focus on praying a prayer but little focus on the heart cry of faith that must accompany that prayer. I had unknowingly been trained that the most important part of the gospel message was getting a person to that point of decision and having them repeat the prayer. I remember the training that we went through to learn how to share the gospel; I will be forever grateful for the emphasis placed on reaching the lost but equally as bothered by the overemphasis on the 'sinners prayer.' I remember saying numerous times, "If you want to be saved just pray this prayer after me." It was so engrained into our 'routine' that the prayer became the mode of salvation as opposed to a heart cry of faith. I'm thankful that my parents had enough discernment and courage to take a stand on such a crucial issue surrounding the gospel.

With all that being said, Scripture does speak of a prayer of the heart in regards to salvation. Romans 10:13 is often used as the foundational text dealing with this issue. "For whosoever shall call upon the name of the Lord shall be saved." In my opinion, no one was as influential in bringing awareness to the concept of a sinners prayer than Billy Graham. He led an estimated 2.2 million people through this prayer at his crusades that reached over 215 million people all across the globe.

"Dear Lord Jesus, I know that I am a sinner, and I ask for Your forgiveness. I believe You died for my sins and rose from the dead. I turn from my sins and invite You to come into my heart and life. I want to trust and follow You as my Lord and Savior. In Your Name. Amen."[16]

Is this what the "sinners prayer" should look like? When a person truly desires to come to Christ in faith, what should the prayer of the heart look like? Step back with me for a few

---

[16] Billy Graham, https://peacewithgod.net (accessed 07/11/2018)

moments, and let's examine what I believe is the closest example of a sinner's prayer that we find in Scripture: the prayer of the prodigal son.

Remember, the foundation for the prodigal son's prayer was established in the previous pages: he recognized his own depravity and knew of the father's ability to save him. With that foundation in place, he prepares for the journey home, knowing that he will have to face the just wrath of the father and a culture that he has scorned through his rebellious actions. His prayer is short and simple. "Father, I have sinned. I am not worthy to be a son. I ask that you would allow me to just be your servant." The prodigal son is communicating some very deep truths in these simple words!

In his prayer, we catch an incredible glimpse into the heart of a repentant sinner. First, he is admitting his own sin. "Father, I have sinned against heaven, and before thee." The heart cry for salvation must involve a recognition of our sinful state; without sin there is no need for a Savior or redemption. Second, he communicates a state of dependence. He is asking the father to do for him what he cannot do for himself. Third, his prayer is a vehicle of humility. "...And am no more worthy to be called thy son:" When a sinner comes to God there can be no pride or pretention. Salvation that is deserved or earned is not Biblical salvation. Finally, the younger son recognized that he did not deserve to be loved and accepted as a son; his request was to be allowed to just live as a servant and nothing more.

What we are witnessing in these verses is the heart cry of a repentant sinner! "God, I know that I am a sinner, and I deserve your wrath. I place myself at your mercy and ask for your grace." As a side note, we know this represents a heart prayer because he isn't standing in front of the father yet. He is all alone in a strange country, recognizing the depths of his despair and inability to save himself. If the prayer for salvation doesn't start in the heart, it is powerless to save; prayers don't save, Jesus Christ saves!

SALVATION IN FOCUS #6 - The Sinner's Prayer

When you are sharing the gospel with an unbeliever and they are at the point of faith, do you skip praying? The answer is no. Prayer is our mode of conversation with God, and the prayer of a repentant sinner is a cause for rejoicing in heaven! However, there are no magic words in Christianity. Becoming a child of God doesn't happen through a repeated set of words or phrases any more than drawing close to God through vain repetitions. When someone comes to their point of faith, the prayer of the sinner becomes a heart cry for mercy and grace. No two people will communicate their heart cry to God the same way. Instead of 'leading them in prayer', allow that person to simply pray to God from their own heart. It's possible they might resist initially. In fact, often they will say "but I don't know what to say!" It is at that point that you lead them away from a recited prayer and lead them toward a prayer of the heart.

Chapter 9
Repentance and Faith

Luke 15:18-20 I will arise and go to my father, and will say unto him, Father, I have sinned against heaven, and before thee, and am no more worthy to be called thy son: make me as one of thy hired servants. And he arose, and came to his father.

Repentance is a cornerstone truth within the salvation discussion. Or is it? Too often it is misunderstood, misapplied, or simply left out of the 'equation' all together. The confusion stems primarily from the presence of repentance in the message of Scripture but its lack of clear definition within those texts. Another issue arises when we conflate repentance and confession as the same, though they are different in terms of their application in Scripture.

Repentance connected with salvation is a primary focus of the preaching of the early church, seen predominantly in the book of Acts. The early church was founded on the clear message of repentance: repentance leads to eternal life, the command to repent, as well as repentance as the turn toward God. (Acts 2:38, 3:19, 11:18, 17:30, 20:21, and 26:20) Often we hear preaching that calls sinners to repentance or prayers of national repentance. Believers may even walk the aisle and in prayer "repent" of their sins (actually meaning confession). I would like us to consider two examples of repentance in the Scriptures, both found in Luke's Gospel.

A simple illustration of repentance can be found in the narrative of Zacchaeus and his interaction with Jesus Christ in Luke 19. Zacchaeus was a tax collector and as a consequence was rich and hated. He was rich in that he skimmed money off the taxes that were collected from fellow Jews; in essence he was stealing from them by collecting too much in taxes. He was hated because no one likes a thief that has the backing and authority of the government! Zacchaeus had heard that Jesus was passing through the area, and because of his short stature, he climbed into a tree to be able to view the procession of the Savior. As our Lord walked by him that day, He looked upward, gazing directly into the eyes of a crooked and prideful Pharisee. "Zacchaeus, make haste, and come down; for to day I must abide at thy house." Without any hesitation, Zacchaeus climbed down and received Jesus into his own home. Of course, as the Pharisees often did, they stood outside grumbling that Jesus would dare to fellowship and eat with someone so unworthy of His time and attention.

We don't know much about Zacchaeus in the Scriptures, but we do know that the time he spent with the Savior prompted a radical change in his life!   "And Zacchaeus stood, and said unto the Lord; Behold, Lord, the half of my goods I give to the poor; and if I have taken any thing from any man by false accusation, I restore him fourfold." The lifestyle that he had lived was in the past. He was a different man with a different outlook on his actions and how they affected others. He literally made a turn away from his old way of living toward a new reality. In essence, he agreed with Jesus that his stealing and dishonest ways were wicked and wrong. That produced a turn away from those things and a turn toward Jesus.

SALVATION IN FOCUS #7 What is repentance?

Repentance is actually a simple Scriptural concept; in our attempt to 'dig deeper' into Scriptural Truth we have made it far more difficult and complex than God's Word affords. To 'repent' (from the Greek μετανοέω - metanoeo) simply means "to reconsider" or "to think differently." It connotes a change of mind that is seen in a change of direction/lifestyle throughout the Gospel record. The story of Zacchaeus perfectly illustrates repentance; his turning away from his sinful lifestyle and his turning toward the path of righteousness is the very repentance that Jesus spoke when He said "except ye repent, ye shall all likewise perish." (Luke 13:5) In Zaccheus's case, he was confronted with the reality of his sin and came to the point where he agreed with Jesus's perspective. This is where we have added confusion. Repentance isn't a separate event that happens during conversion. It is an integral part of the turning from sin and toward God!

The second illustration of repentance is plainly found within our text. The prodigal son perfectly demonstrates the repentance of a heart that turns from sin and toward grace of the loving father. As we have seen in previous chapters, this point in the story finds him an outcast of the father, apart from his provision, and living in the squalor of his sin. He is helpless and hopeless. We read, however, of the moment that he comes to himself. There is a recognition of the desperation of his condition and the wonderful provision that is available through the father. Why is his condition so desperate? Because he had followed his own path—the pathway of rebellion always leads us down the road to destruction.

To really see the repentance of the younger son we have to see the radical turn that he was making through this move toward home. What was the old 'plan'?

1. Give me the portion of goods that belongs to me.
2. I reject you and choose to go my own way.
3. Life is about my pleasure and sinful satisfaction.
4. There is a famine? I can save myself! (I just need a job…I

can handle this.)

Now compare that to the new 'plan' that he sets forth in these verses:
1. I recognize my sin.
2. I realize that my sin has caused my separation from the father.
3. My circumstances are my own fault.
4. I am helpless without the grace of the father.
5. I am unworthy of any goodness from the father.

Do you notice how he was going one way with his life choices and made a full 180 degree turn! The prodigal son actually gives us an incredible insight into what happened in the heart of Zacchaeus when he met the Savior. Before he was a cheat and thief. Afterward, he restored what he had taken fourfold and began a life of looking toward others and not himself. As the younger son made his turn toward home, he demonstrates an incredible truth about the salvation of mankind: the necessity of repentance.

If you have ever wanted to know what repentance looks like....we just saw an incredible illustration! It is relatively easy to see the prodigal son make the turn toward home and away from his sinful state. Please understand, though, the turn away from his sin did not restore him to his father's fellowship — it was the gracious work of the father. Period. There was no goodness seen in the son's turn toward home, only his inability to save himself from the chaos his decisions had created. His repentance demonstrated another very important aspect of our salvation that functions as a beautiful complement. Repentance demands a focus, a pivot on which 'the turn' takes place. This wonderful counterpart is faith!

Sit under the preaching of 10 different pastors, and you will hear 10 different calls to respond: repent, submit, believe, come, pray. We see the same pattern in the Gospels. When John the Baptist was preaching in the wilderness of Judea, his call to respond was simple: "Repent ye: for the kingdom of heaven is at hand." (Matthew 3:1-3) Peter seemed to preach the same message while urging the listeners at Pentecost to "Repent, and be baptized every one of you in the name of Jesus Christ for the remission of sins." (Luke 2:38) Paul's message to the Athenians seems to be in parallel with the previous examples as he commanded "all men every where to repent:" (Acts 17:30)

On the other hand, we often hear a call to believe as well. For example, in Acts 16 Paul and Silas are in prison as the angel causes an earthquake and the doors to open. The jailor, thinking that all the prisoners had escaped, looks down the sharp end of his sword and is moments away from taking his life. Paul and Silas assure him that they are still there; he is overwhelmed with emotion and conviction. "Sirs, what must I do to be saved?" Paul's answer is simple. "Believe on the Lord Jesus Christ, and thou shalt be saved, and thy house." (Acts 16:31) In

Acts 17 we see that Paul not only told the Athenians to repent but goes on to describe them as those that believed. Were Paul's own words in contradiction to his own teaching? Which is it? Repent or believe?

All of the confusion is made clear when we consider the words of our Savior; His words are straightforward and authoritative. "The time is fulfilled, and the kingdom of God is at hand: <u>repent</u> ye, and <u>believe</u> the gospel." (Mark 1:15) Notice how Jesus put both together! Both repentance and belief are essential to salvation. In a sense, repentance and faith are closely connected and function as two sides to the same coin. Faith demands a turn from the path of sin, and the turn toward the father's grace demands faith in the Father's ability to rescue! Neither can exist without the other! It is clear that faith and repentance cannot happen without the other - they can't be separated!

In essence, repentance and faith are the same action but from a different perspective. From God's perspective, the turn of faith is seen in my willingness to accept my sin for what it is and to agree with God that the only way to obtain salvation is through Jesus Christ. From man's perspective, as we turn from our sin and agree with God about our sinful state, there must be a focus to which we turn; there must be an object on which we set our spiritual gaze. That focus is a faith in Christ and his free offer of redemption!

This brings up another issue that surrounds repentance and faith...one which causes unnecessary conflict within the salvation framework. This issue is summed up in a question: Does the repentance/faith action constitute a 'work' that detracts from the free mercy and grace of redemption? The claim set forth by some is that the 'action' of repentance and faith should be regarded as a work; a work that detracts from the glory of God by somehow creating a condition where salvation is now earned through that repentance and faith and is no longer a free gift. Since we know from Scripture that salvation is not earned but is freely given, then repentance and faith cannot be the means by which salvation is received; if so, then salvation would be earned by works. Often Ephesians 2:8-9 will be used to support this position, though it requires an awkward reading of the text as well as the neglect of other clear passages in the New Testament.

> **For by grace are ye saved through faith; and that not of yourselves: it is the gift of God: Not of works, lest any man should boast.**

Let's summarize what Paul is saying.
- We are saved by grace (God's unmerited favor/redemption) through (or by means of) faith (the trust we place in God to forgive and restore).
- It is not of ourselves. There is no work that can earn salvation.
- It is the gift of God. What is the gift of God? Is faith

> the gift? Is salvation the gift?
- Still talking about the 'it', it is not of works or else we would boast and be puffed up with pride.

The question comes down to this...what is the 'it' referring to? This is of utmost importance to our framework of salvation! Let's consider the two options. Option one is that salvation is the gift. This would establish that man is responsible to repent and believe in the message of salvation, and God (in His sovereignty) chooses to grant salvation on those grounds. Option two is that faith itself is the gift. Man in his sin has no ability to respond to the free offer of salvation and must wait for the quickening of the spirit before he can repent. In this framework, there is no repentance or faith needed for salvation on the part of a sinner; the irresistible moving of the Holy Spirit actually 'awakens' the soul and brings about regeneration prior to any repentance or faith.

Compare these two 'options' to the text that is set before us in Luke 15. Remember, this text is the greatest illustration of salvation given to man and was given directly from Jesus Christ Himself. We should make the assumption that Jesus knew what He was talking about and was intentional in how He crafted this story! (said in slight sarcasm) With that in mind, let us consider which of these two options matches the salvation that our Savior set before us.

We will start with option two. In this framework, we should see the young outcast in the fields feeding the swine. Unknown to him, his father has made the journey from the village to meet him in the field. The son has no knowledge of the father's desire to offer grace, and frankly, the son has no desire to go home at all and restore the fellowship that has been broken. He is loving his life with the pigs! He is dead to the father with no awareness of the desperation of his situation. And then it happens. Suddenly, the son feels a stiff hand on his shoulder. He turns to see his father with a rope, a restraint to bind the son against his will and drag him home. This isn't what he wanted; he loves feeding and lounging with the pigs! The scene ends with the son tied up in the restraints and being forced onto the wagon. He is headed home. Dad is dragging him home against his will.

Does option number two describe the illustration that Jesus chose to demonstrate salvation? It does not take much more than a cursory glimpse at our parable to realize that option two, the idea that regeneration proceeds repentance and faith, stands in direct conflict with Christ's teaching. Rather, what we see in this parable is that the son comes to himself. We see him recognizing the helplessness of his sinful condition and the hope that is found in the father. We see the son changing his mind and agreeing with the father about his guilt. We see the son demonstrating a faith in the father to meet the need and save him from his circumstances. We see the son turning to the father in full reliance and faith. Does this in any way mean that he has earned his restoration? Does his repentance and faith constitute a work that has earned the father's mercy?

Absolutely not. This repentance and faith dynamic is beautifully worded in the hymn, Rock of Ages, written by Augustus Toplady in 1763.

> Nothing in my hands I bring,
> Simply to thy cross I cling;
> Naked, come to thee for dress.
> Helpless, look to thee for grace.
> Foul, I to the fountain fly,
> Wash me, Savior, or I die.

SALVATION IN FOCUS #8 What is saving faith?

What is saving faith? When a person hears the convicting message of the gospel, is it enough for that person to just consent to the gospel? The answer is no. James speaks of this in his epistle. James 2:19 states, "Thou believest that there is one God; thou doest well: the devils also believe, and tremble." Even the demons have a knowledge of the Savior. In Job we see Satan himself approaching, interacting, and communicating with God. It is clear that a head knowledge of truth is not enough to save any more that the prodigal son's knowledge of the father was enough to restore him to sonship while he remained with the pigs. Faith is best seen in the actions of the heroes of the faith from Hebrews 11. These individuals heard the words of God and then acted in obedience, trusting that

God would follow through with His words. The Greek word for faith (πίστις pistis) means full reliance or belief. Faith, in other words, is putting your trust in God to do what He has promised in His Word. Though we can have 'faith' in many areas of life, saving faith is the confidence that the Savior has both the means and the ability to restore your broken spirit. The prodigal son voiced saving faith with these words:

Father, I have sinned against heaven, and before thee, and am no more worthy to be called thy son: make me as one of thy hired servants.

As we conclude our discussion on repentance and faith, we must address one last issue that surrounds repentance and faith: Is repentance necessary for salvation? You might think this would be a long discussion that would need its own chapter. The reality is we have laid the groundwork that should guide us fairly quickly to a conclusion from Scripture.

The first thing we see from God's Word is that you cannot repent without truly believing, and you cannot truly believe in the Gospel without repenting. Though they are not the same thing, repentance and faith represent two sides of the same coin...you can't have one without the other. II Timothy 2:25 ties the two beautifully together as it describes "repentance to the acknowledging of truth." Paul describes his witness to the Greeks as preaching "repentance toward God, and faith toward our Lord Jesus Christ." (Acts 20:21) Another way to regard the connection is with this truth in mind: a penitent heart turns away from sin and toward God. There must be a new object of attraction for a repentant sinner's heart. If repentance is the turn away from sin in agreement with God, then the turn toward God for salvation is the belief in God's ability to save. The prodigal son could not have turned toward the father if he had not at the same time turned away from his helpless condition.

The confusion often comes when people think it is repentance plus faith or faith plus repentance. Rather, it is faith that repents. Salvation demands a repentant faith.

Chapter 10
The Father Ran

Let us pause for a moment and reflect back to the context of this parable; Christ is using the story of the rebellious/lost son to expose the coldness to the gospel within the heart of the Pharisees. He has masterfully woven together cultural and community connections that have made the story colorful and deep; these cutlural associations also create a connection emotionally to the events that are unfolding. To a parent that has tragically lost a child, a story about a child that perishes would stir up deep emotions. To a spouse that has been the victim of unfaithfulness, a story of adultery would bring up intense feelings and create a certain heart reaction. To a pharisee that is steeped in the law and cutural appropriateness, the story that Jesus has crafted has drawn them in and set them up for a bitter moment of truth.

At this point in the parable, there would have been feelings of anger and hatred toward the rebellious son. His disregard for the father was despicable and heinous. As Christ unfolds the son's demise, it would have been satisfying for them to see his 'rock bottom' moment unfold. Why? Because he deserved to be at rock bottom! He deserved to be an outcast. He had turned his back on his family and community; to see him starving, begging, and feeding the pigs was a fitting end to a son that had acted as he had. Vulnerable, exposed, and empty: the pharisees's anger would have been appeased to see the younger son come to these ends.

It was equally satisfying to see the son admit how powerless he was to save himself. As Christ verbalized the son's 'come to himself' moment, there would have been an overwhelming sense of noble justice in their minds. Not only did he end up with the pigs, he realized that it was his fault, and his only recourse was to come home begging. In the prodigal son's prayer he stated that he was unworthy to be called a son. He was begging to be reinstated as a slave with no rights as a son. The Pharisees would have agreed wholeheartedly!

What happened next, however, would have taken them completely off guard. In a sense, Jesus had set them up perfectly by slightly putting their hearts at ease. He had brought them to a point in the story where the conclusion was in sight and yet included a turn of events so offensive to their culture that the entire balance of the parable rested on these verses. Before we consider what was exceedingly offensive, can we guess how the parable should have ended at this point to satisfy the Pharisee's sense of cultural justice?

The younger son comes to himself and realizes that his only recourse is to admit full guilt and beg for the father's mercy.

The cultural expectation was simple: no mercy. Incredible shame had been brought on the family by the son's actions; honor had to be restored. The son must be brought to shame by the father and shunned by the community. In fact, the father might not even be the first one to deal with the shame upon the son's arrival back home. It was quite common for the community to rally around the shamed family and act on their behalf to restore honor. Not only did the culture recognize this type of 'justice' as appropriate, there were Biblical laws on rebellion as well. As this young man was preparing to walk back into town to beg for mercy, the Pharisees were mentally preparing for him to be shunned, shamed, and possibly stoned for his rebellious actions. In their minds, this would be the fitting end for Christ's story. Instead, a shocking turn of events was in store.

Luke 15:20 And he arose, and came to his father. But when he was yet a great way off, his father saw him, and had compassion, and ran, and fell on his neck, and kissed him.

This was not the reaction that the Pharisees were looking for; there was an insatiable appetite for cultural resolution, and this did not satisfy that appetite! Though this was just a story, Christ had woven in such intricate cultural connections that they couldn't help but be drawn into the emotion of the moment. The son did not deserve the Father's mercy! We know this was their reaction because this was the very spiritual response that the Pharisees were guilty of and our Savior was aiming to point out through this parable. There was a desire to see sinners pushed away from the love of our Savior. Sinners did not deserve his time and attention. The Pharisees would become angry and secretly murmur at the favor being shown to an undeserving class of people. Their case was simple; there was no other groundwork needed other than to make the cultural claim against our Lord. Luke 15:2 states that the "scribes murmured, saying, This man receiveth sinners, and eateth with them." No evidence was needed and no futher explanation was required. The receiving of sinners was a violation of their code of morality. In the same sense, the receiving of the son would have been equally as offensive to their cultural morality. This was accentuated by the fact that the father was eagerly waiting the son's return!

There are a few interesting thoughts about this portion of the parable. To begin with, Christ describes the father as seeing him (the returning son) a great way off. The passage clearly communicates an anticipation that the son will return, and the father is waiting, longing for the restored fellowship with his wayward child! This wasn't a forced return, either. The son had to come to himself. Just to be clear, the father in our story had ample resources to go and retrieve his son by force. He could have sent a convoy of servants to find his wayward child and irresistibly bring him back home. The father himself could have met the son in the field and commanded that he return. Culturally, the father could have demanded his son to return and the father's wishes would have been carried out. That, however, is not the picture that our Lord paints of the father's love. Rather, we see that the father's love is patient, anticipating that the son will "come to himself" as is described in the previous verses.

Some would say that this view of the father (the Savior) dimishes his soveriegnty and power. They would state that in order to be sovereign, God must actively decree all that will come to pass and that nothing happens that He has not ordained. This clearly does not fit the teaching on salvation that Jesus gives. This view of sovereignty, however, is the basis for a soteriological view that demands that Christ reach into the soul of the unsaved and breath spiritual life into him, completely apart from faith and repentance. Is this really what the Father's sovereign love looks like? I think it is time we shed light on the Biblical understanding of sovereignty.

First, we need to understand the simple definition. Though many exist, all follow along this common thread; sovereignty is the state of having supreme authority in position and power, demonstrated in the authority of a king. In fact, the word actually is derived from the English root word *soverain* which is the noun basis for king, monarch, or supreme ruler. To fully understand how the word is correctly used in our language, we need to grasp a very important concept. Don't bail on me. It's time for a short English lesson. Consider these two sentences about Richard I (The Lionhearted), King of England from 1189 - 1199 bc.

1. Richard is powerful.
2. Richard is king.

In both sentences Richard is the subject; the sentence is obviously about him. In both sentences the word 'is' functions as a linking verb, linking the word that follows with the subject of the sentence. This is where the two sentences part ways. In the sentence "Richard is powerful", *powerful* acts as a predicate adjective, describing Richard and helping us to understand the attributes of Richard. In the second sentence, "Richard is king," the word *king* functions as a predicate noun. It doesn't describe an attribute but renames Richard. Richard isn't *kingly*, rather Richard *is* king! You could apply the 'equals' test to each case to help see the difference. Richard is powerful. Is Richard equal to powerful? No. Richard is king. Is Richard equal to king? Yes! A predicate noun renames the subject and can be used in it's place, in the same way that a servant could approach King Richard I and directly call him 'King.'

Now, let's consider this statement: God is sovereign. As we learned, the word sovereign must act as either a predicate adjective or a predicate noun. Either it describes an attribute of God, or it renames God. One or the other. If sovereign functions as an adjective, then it tells us of God's power and authority as king. If sovereign functions as a noun, then it declares this truth; God is king. Which one is correct? Well,

Scripture is overwhelming in its answer. God is Sovereign...God is King of Kings! While it isn't wrong to say that God is powerful (He obviously is all powerful - omnipotent is the theological adjective to describe that aspect of His being), it is inconsistent with the usage in Scripture to primarily use "sovereign" as an adjective. Unfortunately, that is exactly how it is primarily used today. Instead of acknowledging God as The Sovereign as King of Kings, God is proclaimed as sovereign in his ability and actions. Sovereignty is being used to describe how he acts instead of who he is. Unfortunately, that simple inconsistency has major doctrinal ramifications.

This may come as a suprise to you, but the words 'sovereign' and 'sovereignty' are not found in the King James Version (KJV) of the Scriptures. Excluding the two times that the word is entered into the text but isn't in the Greek text, the English Standard Version (ESV) only has one use of the word found in I Timothy 6:15. While the New International Version (NIV) does use the word sovereign over 300 times in the Old Testament, it is always used in association with the title "Lord" and is equivalent to the KJV title of "Lord God." The closest Greek word in the New Testament is (βασιλεύς) *basileus* which is found 118 times in the Textus Receptus. All 118 times is is translated as king (noun). It is not describing in what way God rules but is actually telling us who He is...He is the King of Kings! <u>Not one single time does the language come anywhere close to the modern usage of the word "sovereign" or what is has come to define.</u> Not once. With that in mind, it is totally in line with the Biblical pattern to refer to God as sovereign, but it is not in line with the Biblical pattern to use sovereignty to define God's attributes.

Sadly, religion has redefined the word "sovereign" and changed its meaning from "God is King of Kings" to "God controls and determines everything." This redefining of God's kingship has resulted in a theological shift that put's God in the drivers seat of all things that happen, including evil and sin. God is reduced from an all-powerful supreme deity that can take even the wicked choices of men and use them to accomplish His good will to a controlling deterministic deity that only wins for eternity because He is playing both sides of the chess board. Is this the relationship that we see between the prodigal son and his father? Christ could have easily crafted this illustration of salvation to demonstrate the deterministic 'sovereignty' that some would hold; instead, we see a father that patiently waits for the son to come to himself and make the turn back toward home.

SALVATION IN FOCUS #9 - Whosoever will may come.

God, as Sovereign, has the authority to choose the criteria by which salvation is graciously given. Is salvation available to "whoseover will" or only to a select few? Are the arms of Jesus open in anticipation of sinners making the turn of repentance, or has God predetermined those who would come in faith and already rejected those that are not one of the chosen? What we see through Jesus's teaching is that the father patiently waits for the son to make the turn as opposed to chasing him down and forcing him irresistably to make the turn toward home. This is also the pattern we see all through Scripture: the gospel is preached, man believes and repents through faith, and then redemption is given by grace.

John 3:15-16 That whosoever believeth in him should not perish, but have eternal life. For God so loved the world, that he gave his only begotten Son, that whosoever believeth in him should not perish, but have everlasting life.

John 12:46 I am come a light into the world, that whosoever believeth on me should not abide in darkness.

Acts 2:21 And it shall come to pass, that whosoever shall call on the name of the Lord shall be saved.

So the passage describes the father as seeing him a great way off, communicating anticipation. The second truth we see is through the first action of the father; he ran to meet his wayward son! Not only was there an anticipation of the son's return, but there was a reaching out to meet him on his journey back home. The father didn't waste any time; he ran with haste to meet his son! This, as well, would be highly exceptional in their culture; men of wealth and means would not stoop themselves to running down the road. There were servants. It was shameful. If the need was great, they would send a servant to do their bidding, send their greeting, or welcome their guests. Not this time. The father pulled up his robe and took off to meet his son! How could this be? In fact, the appropriate cultural reaction would have been to react in anger. The father should have refused to meet the son! There was no honor in running to meet a rebellious child; instead the father brought shame upon himself.

Romans 5:7-8 7 For scarcely for a righteous man will one die: yet peradventure for a good man some would even dare to die. 8 But God commendeth his love toward us, in that, while we were yet sinners, Christ died for us.

While this may seem like a small part of the reunion story, there is an incredible truth that is illustrated through the father's hurried dash to meet the son. To grasp that truth we have to remember the intense cloud of shame that the son left under. Having turned his back on his family, his father, and his culture, the son walked away in rebellious defiance. The shame and embarassment of the family and the community would have rippled outward into the countryside; the son left in a way that he could never return home. To walk back into town would bring harsh and swift 'justice' at the hands of the angry community. He did not deserve to be a son. Nothing would change that reality.

Nothing would change that reality except the humble and compassionate actions of the father. The father didn't just run because he was full of excitement; he ran to protect his son from the harsh reaction of an angry community. In essence, the father took the shame of the son on himself. I am reminded of Hebrews 12:2 which states "Looking unto Jesus the author and finisher of our faith; who for the joy that was set before him endured the cross, despising the shame, and is set down at the right hand of the throne of God." Jesus endured the cross and took upon him the shame of our sin. He took our shame so that we could be brought back into fellowship with God!

SALVATION IN FOCUS #10 - He bore our shame.

This 'shame' that the father took on himself is critical to the acceptance of the son back into the community; someone had to bear the shame, and it was the father. Someone had to bear the shame for our sin, and it was the Savior! There was nothing the son could do to right his wrongs, and there is nothing we can do to make amends for our sin either. It took the sacrifice of the spotless lamb of God to assuage the wrath of the Righteous Judge.

> **Philippians 2:4-8 4 Look not every man on his own things, but every man also on the things of others. 5 Let this mind be in you, which was also in Christ Jesus: 6 Who, being in the form of God, thought it not robbery to be equal with God: 7 But made himself of no reputation, and took upon him the form of a servant, and was made in the likeness of men: 8 And being found in fashion as a man, he humbled himself, and became obedient unto death, even the death of the cross.**

From our cultural perspective, this part of the story is simply breathtaking. To see the father patiently waiting for the return of the wayward son is such a beautiful picture of compassion and mercy! The son deserved nothing but shame and rejection and yet the father gives him only kindness and sympathy. Our culture rejoices in undeserved kindness; if there ever was an undeserving son, it was this young man! The father's unexpected reaction to the son is evidenced through the use of a very colorful word that helps us to see what was going on inside the father's emotions; the father was moved with compassion.

What exactly is compassion? Is it mercy? Is it grace? It

actually goes much deeper that those and is best understood when we see that the Greek word from which it is translated (σπλαγχνίζομαι splagchnizomai) literally means "to yearn deep in the bowels." This is a feeling of care and concern that touches you on the inside. This level of compassion is driven by a deep sense of love and empathy; it occurs when the emotional concern is so deep that it crosses over to the physical. Picture a mother clutching the motionless hand of her only son as the doctors work frantically to revive him. Countless books and movies have centered around the deep-seated emotional reaction that a parent has for their hurting child. Our culture glories in love that deep! The father's compassion was so deep that he was moved to empty himself of pride. There was no holding back the outward show of his inward compassion as he dropped his outer garment and began running with outstretched arms toward his returning son. In fact, he was so focused on the happy reunion, that he offered forgiveness and reconciliation before the son had said one single word!

From our cultural perspective, this part of the story is breathtaking. To the Pharisees, however, this would have been viewed much differently. There was no honor in forgiveness. There was honor in reconciliation. This story was not going the way they thought it would.

...a note from the author...

Future Plans: As you can see, a proper understanding of God and his position as Sovereign is important to understanding his interactions with mankind. Though I have a few other books already in their beginning stages, I plan on addressing this at some point in the future. If you are interested in receiving a notification when that book is complete, go to www.djharry.org/connect and sign up. Many that sign up will also receive an advanced reader copy before it it published!

Chapter 11
Sonship Restored

Luke 15:22-24 But the father said to his servants, Bring forth the best robe, and put it on him; and put a ring on his hand, and shoes on his feet: And bring hither the fatted calf, and kill it; and let us eat, and be merry: For this my son was dead, and is alive again; he was lost, and is found. And they began to be merry.

As we just saw, the Pharisee's reaction to the events so far would be pure astonishment. There was no room in their culture for the father to offer forgiveness like he did. The shame that the father took on himself was unprecedented; the son deserved to suffer considerable shame for the dishonor he had brought on the family name. Instead of shame, though, the father responds with undeserved grace. There are two definitions of grace that have stuck with me through the years.

The first is an acronym of the word grace: God's Riches At Christ's Expense. This definition describes the favor that our God demonstrated through Jesus on the cross and is specific to salvation. To understand grace, though, it is helpful to look at the second definition: God's unmerited favor.

We see two examples of grace in this part of the passage and each are undeserved and coming from the father. First, the father gives the son what can only be described as a hero's arrival! It was a "spare no expense" and "no holds barred" kind of reception that the son received right there in front of his house. We haven't even made it to the real celebration, and the father is snapping out orders to bring out the best clothing, the family jewelry, and to make ready for a family feast. There was no hesitation in the father's welcome; it was immediate and complete!

The second act of grace that we see in this passage is that the son that was dead, the one that had been disowned and had walked away in shame, was immediately restored to the position of sonship. With no expectation of an explanation and without any hesitancy, the father announces to the entire village that "this my son was dead, and is alive again." It is hard, even in our culture, to comprehend this act of grace and immediate restoration. Surely the son had "some explaining to do!" Most fathers in this circumstance would have demanded an explanation or at least set some ground rules for the son to return. Do you remember the son's prayer to his father? Even he recognized that he didn't deserve to be called a son and so he only requested to be a servant. Sonship was out of the question! Sonship would be the ultimate demonstration of unmerited favor from the father.

SALVATION IN FOCUS #11 - Immediate Sonship

In the same way that the prodigal son was immediately granted all the rights and priviledges of sonship, God immediately grants to sinners the position of sonship at the point of salvation. Consider what Paul states in Galatians 3:6-7. "Even as Abraham believed God, and it was accounted to him for righteousness. Know ye therefore that they which are of faith, the same are the children of Abraham." Paul is clear that the adoption of sons comes at the point of regeneration, a result of saving faith and a heart of repentance. Paul goes on in verse 26 to say, "For ye are all the children of God by faith in Christ Jesus." Sonship is immediate and complete. There is no middle ground where sonship is earned…it is a gift freely given!

A robe. A ring. Shoes. The fatted calf. These are four items that mean very little to our culture, but to the audience of Jesus they each had a unique place in society and culture. To us it would be like a boy/young man waking up on the day that he turns 18 years old to find a key ring with a solitary key sitting on his dresser. As the energetic 18 year old runs with excitement, he opens the door to find that mom and dad have bought him the greatest gift a 18 year old could get...his own car! It represents independence and maturity, responsibility and ownership. It might look like a pile of nuts and bolts to those driving by, but to this young man it is the most beautiful car he has ever laid eyes on...because it is his!

Gifts have cultural meaning. To us, a car represents independence. Clothes represent growth. Toys tell us of youth. Flowers tell us of love. Jewelry demonstrates commitment. A lump of coal or an old fruitcake means that you have friends with a great sense of humor! No matter the gift, we walk away from opening a present and recognize that it has communicated something about the relationship between the giver and the receiver. It was no different in Jesus's day; the giving of gifts had significance. Could it be that each of the gifts that Jesus listed was given on purpose and had significance within the parable? With a little study we see that each item had a purpose in their culture and Jesus was communicating truth through those items.

First, the father calls for the servants to bring forth the "best robe." When we see the word 'best' we can actually come to different conclusions based on what we think is best. Is cleanest best? Is most expensive best? Is most ornate best? Rather, the Greek word for best means the 'formost in importance' or 'chief'. It wasn't just an important jacket or important headdress, it was the foremost robe in the house that was a mark of dignity. What robe in the house would have been the 'best robe' other than the father's own robe? Imagine the servants slowly opening up their master's closet and removing his best robe to bring out and place on the returning son. Pause for a moment and remember that each part of this parable is given as a parallel of how God relates to a sinner that comes to repentance. This just might be the most beautiful picture of our salvation in the entire parable! At salvation, Christ placed his righteousness over my sinful flesh so that in God's eyes I stand justified!

> *His robes for mine: O wonderful exchange!*
> *Clothed in my sin, Christ suffered 'neath God's rage.*
> *Draped in His righteousness, I'm justified.*
> *In Christ I live, for in my place He died.*[17]

The second gift that the father gives is a ring. I'm pretty sure that we see at least some significance with the ring; even our culture values the personal gift of jewelry. A ring in their culture didn't so much signify the relationship as much as it demonstrated authority. Rings, or signets, were worn by those in authority and communicated their total command. We see this illustrated in Genesis 41 when Pharaoh took the ring off his own finger and gave it to Joseph. It wasn't a gift of kindness or a

---

[17] Anderson, Chris. His Robes for Mine. Copyright 2008, ChurchWorksMedia.com

display of friendship; in that moment, Pharaoh elevated Joseph from a common prisoner to ruler over all the land of Egypt. We see the exact same thing happen in Esther 8 when the king gave his ring to Mordecai. Mordecai was lifted up in authority and was given the power to rule in the king's stead. The ring wasn't decoration - it was authority! When the prodigal son put out his hand and received the ring of the father, he was given all the authority entitled to a son. He was not a servant or a slave as he had requested; all the power of the father was now available to the son through this one gift.

The third gift was shoes. This one is probably the most difficult to understand because shoes have taken on such a different role for us in our culture. We take for granted that we will have shoes for our feet. Other than a child that is running barefoot because he hates wearing shoes, it is pretty abnormal for us to see people walking barefoot in our American culture. The son likely returned wearing no shoes with his feet bare to the elements; this was common among the poor and desperate in their culture. Shoes are just a need. The shoes from this passage were probably just sandals and most likely weren't anything more. Nothing more than a simple need. The lesson from the shoes is simple - God sees the needs of the sinner and treats them with mercy and love.

Finally, the father calls for the fatted calf! The first-century Palestinian diet rarely included meat. It's not that they didn't eat meat just that it was reserved for special occasions. Historic and literary evidence points to a society that centered around food such as grain, dried fruits, vegetables and fish. As we see later in the story, the older son and many of the servants were out in the fields tending to the crops. This is what we would expect them to be doing as opposed to tending herds. This is a calf, then, that is being 'fattened' for a special celebration...and a special celebration has been declared!

This brings us to a very interesting and yet crucial word definition from our text. In fact, it is a phrase from our story that is often taken out of context, even though the word is never used within the text of the parable at all! Are you confused? Well, we have referred to the younger son as the "prodigal son" with regularity, and the parable itself bears that title. Countless times we have referred to a wayward child as a "prodigal son" in the context of his rebellion and defiance to his parents. Sit down and take a deep breath. "Prodigal" has nothing to do with defiance! The word prodigal means "characterized by profuse or wasteful expenditure : lavish."[18] Did you notice that there is no mention of rebellion? The prodigal nature of the younger son was not connected at all to how he treated his father; it is a description of his wastefulness and exorbitant spending.

With that in mind, there are actually two people in this text that are prodigal. Obviously the younger son is wasteful in how

---

[18] https://www.merriam-webster.com/dictionary/prodigal

he squandered the family inheritance. The father, though, is equally as prodigal! Can you imagine referring to this as the "Parable of the Prodigal Father?" It could be called that! As we saw in the previous pages, the father was lavish in his response to the son's return, sparing no expense to bring out the best gifts and a massive feast to celebrate his return. We know this for two reasons. First, it is clear in the story that the father overwhelmed his son with compassion and mercy as he bestowed to him all the rights of sonship. Secondly, when we step back and remember the big picture, this fits exactly what Jesus was trying to communicate within the text. There is extravagant rejoicing in heaven over one sinner that comes to repentance in the same way that the father held nothing back as he rejoiced over the return of his son.

What was the cause of this great celebration? What was the focus of the father's prodigal celebration? Jesus describes the son's return from two different perspectives, both giving incredible insight into the condition of man before salvation and after. First, the father says that his son was "dead" and is now "alive." Second, he describes the son as "lost" and now "found." Since these each describe a sinner before and after salvation, we know that they are parallel illustrations. What does it mean for a sinner to be dead and lost? How about alive and found?

The "deadness" of the sinner has been a point of serious

dispute over the years. Some would say that the state of being "dead in trespasses and sins" (Ephesians 2:1) means that the soul without Christ is incapable of responding to the Gospel and unable to even hear the call to repentance. "Dead men can't hear and dead men can't respond." In essence, the "deadness" of a sinner and his inability to respond the gospel spiritually is based on our understanding of the word "dead" in a physical sense. Often proponents of this position will turn to John 11 and 12 and refer to the story of Lazarus; John declares Lazarus dead (physically) and he is obviously unable to respond until the Lord spoke life into his dead body. The connection between Ephesians (dead in trespasses and sins) adn John 11 and 12 (Lazarus was dead and unable to respond) is with the Greek word νεκρός (nekros) which means "dead." Paul and John use the same word to describe the physical death of Lazarus and the spiritually dead state of a sinful soul. In the same way that Lazarus was unable to respond, a sinful soul is 'dead' spiritually and unable to respond to the call of the gospel. Case closed.

Or is it? There are two very compelling reasons why this argument demonstrates poor hermeneutics as well as establishes this 'truth' on faulty logic. First, to say that Lazarus's physical death and a sinner's spiritual death are equal ignores one very glaring difference — they are not the same! Not the same by a long shot! To base a spiritual doctrine of salvation on a physical miracle of resurrection is to conflate two very different events that happen on two very separate realms of existence. In fact, we are pursuaded all through the Scriptures that our physical existence is temporal, secondary, and trivial compared to the weight of spiritual and eternal matters. To base our understanding of something so fundamental as salvation on a physical miracle of resurrection is poor argumentation and shallow theology. Coupled with that truth is stated purpose of Lazarus's resurrection: the demonstration of the bodily resurrection to come. Jesus used the death of his physical body coupled with his physical resurrection in front of all those witnesses to demonstrate Christ's power over death and the joy of the future bodily resurrection of believers. It was a physical death…accompanied by a physical resurrection…to demonstrate Christ's power over the physical realm.

The second reason why the 'Lazarus argument' is a poor argument and easily set aside is the fact that the same Greek word (νεκρός - nekros) is used elsewhere in Scripture and carries a completely different meaning. Well, not different in that it no longer means "no longer alive" as most dictionaries would state. It is used differently in that it is used in a spiritual context and is given with a more clear explanation than using the Lazarus passage. In fact, let's consider Luke 15:23-24 which state, "And bring hither the fatted calf, and kill it; and let us eat, and be merry: For this my son was dead, and is alive again; he was lost, and is found. And they began to be merry." Since the stated purpose of this parable was to illustrate salvation and the lost coming to repentence, it makes much more sense to allow

Jesus's own teaching to illumine our understanding of what spiritual death looks like! Does spiritually dead mean "unable to respond?" Are those that are "dead in their trespasses and sins" numb to the gospel and lifeless in their ability to hear and turn by faith to the graces of the Father? The answer is 'no.' To fully understand what spiritual death looks like, we have to look no further than the 'dead' son in our story.

Let's ask this question: was the younger son dead? Clearly 'yes!' Yes, the son was dead in that he had been disowned, separated from the father, living in rebellion, and cast aside by his community. In fact, he is declared dead twice by his father! On the other hand, the son was not dead as in "unable to respond." In fact, we spent a good deal of time familiarizing ourselves with the "came to himself" moment and clearly saw that the son, knowing his helplessness and the fathers gracious means, was fully capable of making the turn toward home! To objectively say that an unsaved soul is incapable of responding to the good news of the father's grace, you would have to change the story! Instead of the son coming to himself while feeding the swine and coming to his senses regarding his hoplessness and the father's abundance, you would have the father journeying to the son in his hardened rebellion and dragging the son all the way back home against his 'dead' will. In essence, the father would be rejoicing that the son had returned, but only because he forced him to against his own will. That doesn't sound like cause for rejoicing to me at all!

Understanding the concept of 'alive' is equally revealing to our discussion. The son coming home received the father's embrace, his gifts of sonship, and was welcomed back into the family. His being 'alive' simply refers to his position in relationship to the father. Was he 'corpselike' before coming home and then miraculously received life that drew him back to the father? Is that what Jesus describes in this illustration of salvation? No. Rather, Jesus describes the son's 'alive' state as being back in fellowship with the father and restored as a son!

SALVATION IN FOCUS #12 - Dead in our Sins

The deadness of a soul is the foundation on which most soteriological systems are built. Pelagius taught that Adam's original sin did not taint human nature and that mankind maintained a mortal will that was able to choose good or evil apart from any work of the Holy Spirit. Augustine responded with a theology that defined man as completely dead/incapable of responding to the call of the Gospel. Remember, though, that the traditional view (held by the earliest church leaders) affirmed the balance between God's sovereignty over creation with the necessity of man's response to the gospel. That is what we see in this parable. Knowing the goodness of the father and his own helplessness, the son made the turn toward home!

Ephesians 2:4-5 But God, who is rich in mercy, for his great love wherewith he loved us, even when we were dead in sins, hath quickened us together with Christ, (by grace ye are saved;)

We interrupt this meaningful conversation for a seemingly meaningless question: which came first, the chicken or the egg? While you may have heard that question in your childhood, it did not originate in your childhood. In fact, philosophers have been asking difficult questions like that for thousands of years. It creates a scenario of 'infinite regress' which defines a problem that keeps going and going no matter how many levels you take it. It is like opening a box that contains another box which contains another one....and so one. It never ends.

Now, let's ask a more relevant question but one that has its own difficulties. Which came first, salvation or the sinner's prayer? We already talked about the prayer of repentance in a previous chapter so we won't visit it again. What we did not talk about was the order in which Jesus presents them within the parable at hand. Consider how they are arranged within the story:

1. The younger son came to himself.
2. He acknowledges his helplessness and the father as his only hope.
3. He arose.
4. The father sees him, has compassion and runs to greet

him with a loving embrace.
5. The son verbalizes the prayer he had rehearsed in his heart.

Which came first: the verbalizing of the sinner's prayer or the loving embrace of the father? You will notice the clear order that Jesus set up as the pattern. The father embraced the son before he had ever uttered one word! What we see is that the son acts on the repentance within his heart, the father embraces him lovingly, and then the son begins to verbalize his humble plea to the father. At that point, however, the father had already welcomed him back into the family. The answer to our initial question is clear in our text, and it is equally as clear throughout Scriptural passages that deal with salvation. It isn't a set of words or verbal utterances that brings about salvation; it is the belief and repentance of the heart. In fact, not once in the Scriptures is a person encouraged to pray to receive the gift of salvation.

This is an issue that can become quite contentious in salvation-centered discussions. On one side, prayer is how our spirit communicates with God. Prayer is verbalizing the cry of the heart. Surely a heart that is crying out in faith will verbalize that faith through a prayer of repentance! These are all true statements that of themselves help us to see how a repentant soul could respond with a cry of faith. The issue, however, is not with the prayer itself. The contention is with this belief: it is the prayer that saves. This is not what the Scriptures teach. What we find in God's Word is that God hears the heart cry of belief! Yes, that is often followed up with a verbalization of that repentance, but it isn't the prayer that saves. It is the the heart of belief that saves!

John's account of Christ's redemptive ministry is infused with the message of the gospel. No where in the New Testament do we find a more clear pathway to salvation than in John's narrative of Jesus and His teachings. Consider John's record of Jesus's teaching and notice the clear emphasis on true belief as the basis for salvation.

John 1:12 But as many as received him, to them gave he power to become the sons of God, even to them that <u>believe</u> on his name:

John 3:18 He that believeth on him is not condemned: but he that <u>believeth</u> not is condemned already, because he hath not <u>believed</u> in the name of the only begotten Son of God.

John 8:24 I said therefore unto you, that ye shall die in your sins: for if ye <u>believe</u> not that I am he, ye shall die in your sins.

John 9:38 And he said, Lord, I <u>believe</u>. And he worshipped him.

John 11:26 And whosoever liveth and <u>believeth</u> in me shall never die. <u>Believest</u> thou this? 27 She saith unto him, Yea, Lord: I <u>believe</u> that thou art the Christ, the Son of God, which should come into the world.

John 19:35 And he that saw it bare record, and his record is true: and he *knoweth that he saith true, that ye might <u>believe</u>.*

And no listing would be complete without John 20:31. This is the most critical verse in understanding John's Gospel because he openly declares the purpose and intent of his record…so that people will see who Jesus is and believe!

John 20:31 But these are written, that ye might <u>believe</u> that Jesus is the Christ, the Son of God; and that <u>believing</u> ye might have life through his name.

It is abundantly clear from God's Word that there is an expectation of belief for salvation, a necessity for repentance to accompany that belief….and nothing more. Whenever we demand that a certain set of words be uttered before sonship is restored we veer from the Scriptural path and have added to God's plan of redemption.

Another very important truth to be examined at this point in the story revolves again around the timing of the story — it concerns the order of the events of salvation. It is summed up in this question… "Does regeneration preceed faith or does faith preceed regeneration?" This is no small matter. In fact this question drives to the heart of the two pathways that we have been studying in this book. Either man hears the gospel and is responsible to respond to the gracious call of redemption, or man is chosen apart from his will to salvation and is regenerated before he even believes the gospel call. The foundation for this contrast is contained in the proper understanding of man's 'deadness' to sin. As we saw just a few pages ago, the younger son was dead and yet able to see the helplessness of his condition. The younger son was both lost and dead and yet fully able to make the turn toward the father. Did either of these restore him to sonship? No! But they were all necessary steps to turn in faith to the father that was waiting with open arms!

Does regeneration preceed faith? For some theological systems the answer must be 'yes.' Again, the foundation of this entire conversation comes down to man's 'deadness' in his sin nature. If man is so dead in his sins that he is completely unable and incapable to responding to the gracious call of the father, then there must be some act of regeneration that 'awakens' the dead soul from its deadness and instills into that soul faith. In essence, apart from the work of that regeneration preceeding man's faith, an unsaved soul is incapable of even acknowledging the desperation of his sin and his need of the Father's grace and mercy. This 'regeneration first' timeline becomes quite contradictory to Scripture upon simple analysis. If regeneration happens first, then the unsaved soul has been passed from death unto life and has been restored to fellowship with the Father without the unsaved soul even knowing it. (That soul is completely unaware of the spiritual struggle for his eternal soul because he is 'so dead in his sins' that he cannot even acknowledge his sinful state.) Then with no ability to refuse the call to faith, that regenerated soul 'chooses' (though he has no choice) to put his faith in Christ for salvation (though he is technically already saved). Consider the words of the late Dr. R.C. Sproul (founder of Ligonier Ministries, theologian, Presbyterian elder, an outspoken proponent of reformed theology).

> The reason we do not cooperate with regenerating grace before it acts upon us and in us is because we cannot. We cannot because we are spiritually dead. We can no more assist the Holy Spirit in the quickening of our souls to spiritual life than Lazarus could help Jesus raise him for the dead.[19]
> More specifically, you were not born again because you exercised faith. In truth, the new birth preceded your

---

[19] https://www.ligonier.org/blog/regeneration-precedes-faith/ (accessed 08/10/2018).

faith and produced it. Saving faith is the fruit of regeneration, not the root of it.[20]

If that is the case, then what is the purpose of saving faith? There is none! Faith is completely removed from the salvation equation because saving regeneration preceeds saving faith. To some, this view is the ultimate standard of 'God's Sovereign control' over salvation. Man plays no part in salvation, even to the extent of removing his abilty to respond or even his need to respond. Is this really what it means for salvation to be "all of God?" Those that hold to a 'regeneration first' salvation would say that any participation that man has in salvation takes away from the glory due the Father. The only way God gets all the glory is if God does all the work (even to the exclusion of saving faith).

So here's the question...does man's ability to respond in faith really put him in the drivers seat? Is it necessary that regeneration preceed faith for God to receive the glory? Let's consider Christ's teaching in this salvation parable. First, the son was lost and dead, but that clearly did not mean he was unable to acknowledge his hopeless

---

[20] https://www.ligonier.org/blog/regeneration-monergistic/ (accessed 08/10/2018).

condition. "He came to himself." Christ's words are fairly straightforward on this matter. Second, the son's actions did not earn him any merits with the father. All he did was admit he was unable to save himself and his father had all the means to do so. This ability of the sinful soul to respond or reject the gospel call is seen all through the New Testament. Third, it is ridiculous to suggest that the son's walk back home took away any of the glory of the father's grace and mercy. You cannot divorce the context of the parable from its cultural setting! The dead younger son could do nothing to bring himself back into the family. He was powerless to restore his sonship. All he could do was acknowledge that it was his sin that had created the separation and throw himself at the mercy of the father. The restoration of the younger son was all of the father. The salvation of a repentant sinner is all of Christ!

SALVATION IN FOCUS #13 - God's Plan, God's Way

God is the author of salvation. God is the architect of redemption. God is the source of salvific grace and mercy. As such, He has the right to design and implement the pathway to redemption in whatever way He sees fit. Period. He can save who He wills, give grace to who He wills, and He can redeem who He wills. God has made it exceptionally clear in Scripture that the ones on which he chooses to show his mercy and grace are those that recognize their helplessness and put their faith in Him! To say that His plan reduces His glory is to say that God got it wrong...that our understanding of what brings Him glory is more important than accepting what he has revealed in His Word! Consider the following words of Scripture which are all within the context of salvation and all present God's plan of redeeming those that put their faith in Him.

- **John 20:31** But these are written, that ye might believe that Jesus is the Christ, the Son of God; and that believing ye might have life through his name.
- **John 1:12** But as many as received him, to them gave he power to become the sons of God, even to them that believe on his name:
- **Galatians 3:26** For ye are all the children of God by faith in Christ Jesus.
- **Ephesians 1:12-13** That we should be to the praise of his glory, who first trusted in Christ. In whom ye also trusted, after that ye heard the word of truth, the gospel of your salvation: in whom also after that ye believed, ye were sealed with that holy Spirit of promise...
- **I Timothy 1:16** Howbeit for this cause I obtained mercy, that in me first Jesus Christ might shew forth all longsuffering, for a pattern to them which should

hereafter believe on him to life everlasting.
- **Acts 16:30-31** And brought them out, and said, Sirs, what must I do to be saved? And they said, Believe on the Lord Jesus Christ, and thou shalt be saved, and thy house.

Consider Paul's response to the Philippian jailor in Acts 16:30-31. If regeneration preceeds faith, then the jailor's question about salvation revealed that regeneration had already taken place! If he was 'dead' and unable to even recognize his sinful state, it only follows that regeneration must have already happened at that point in the narrative. Paul's answer should have been "You don't need to do anything…you are already saved!" Instead, Paul sees a man that wants to know more — he sees a lost soul that recognizes he is in need of a Saviour! Paul's response? Believe!

This would seem to bring us to the second break in the story…one which could be an ending itself. Remember, the Pharisees and others listening did not know what direction Jesus was going as he presented this illustration of salvation and rejoicing; they were surprised with every twist and turn that Jesus injected into the story. The first natural break in the story came when the son 'came to himself' and recognized the shame that he had brought onto the family. In their culture, that would have been an instinctive break because it would have ended the story with the son getting what he deserved, chased down by the circumstantial hand of Jehovah and dwelling at the bottom of all humanity.

As we move toward the end of the second major section of the parable, we find the father throwing a celebration that would put most of our parties to shame. There was BBQ, there was music and dancing…it was quite the community celebration! Interestingly, celebrations of this type were not normal in their culture. They did celebrate special events and would happily celebrate the return of a hero or honorable son. They would not, however, celebrate the return of a rebellious child, nor would they find the behavior of the father acceptable. This was completely unconventional and was no doubt confusing for the Pharisees that were listening to Christ's teaching. It is at this celebration, however, that our story finds us at the second natural ending. The son has returned home. Though the father has resolved the shame in an unorthodox manner, honor has been restored through the gracious behavior of the father. The community has come together to celebrate the son's return. Everyone is thrilled with the son's return!

Everyone except the older brother.

Chapter 12
The Elder Son

Luke 15:25-30 Now his elder son was in the field: and as he came and drew nigh to the house, he heard musick and dancing. And he called one of the servants, and asked what these things meant. And he said unto him, Thy brother is come; and thy father hath killed the fatted calf, because he hath received him safe and sound. And he was angry, and would not go in: therefore came his father out, and intreated him. And he answering said to his father, Lo, these many years do I serve thee, neither transgressed I at any time thy commandment: and yet thou never gavest me a kid, that I might make merry with my friends: But as soon as this thy son was come, which hath devoured thy living with harlots, thou hast killed for him the fatted calf.

Near and yet far. There is a parodox in relationships that it is possible to be near to a person in proximity and yet to be far from them emotionally. Sadly, we have all seen this within the marriage relationship; a couple can be living together as husband and wife and yet grow distant to the point that they might say "I don't even know my spouse." A child can spend 16-18 years of their life under their parent's roof and then walk away at age 18 as if the relationship was only a business transaction.

Jesus addresses this exact situation in Matthew 7:21-23. He declared that there will be many that will stand before Him in the day of judgment and will proclaim "Lord, Lord, have we not prophesied in thy name? and in thy name have cast out devils? and in thy name done many wonderful works?" These are people that are involved in church, meeting the needs of the poor and proclaiming their faith in Jesus. Even among that group of 'faithful followers' there will be those that are near to Jesus in action and yet have completely missed out on the reality of saving faith.

There is a reason why Jesus is using an example of a son that is near to the father and yet distant in relationship; the Pharisees had all the advantage of the law and the prophets and yet missed out on having a real relationship with the Messiah. Paul declares this in Romans 3 when he states "What advantage then hath the Jew? or what profit is there of circumcision? Much every way: chiefly, because that unto them were committed the oracles of God." The Jewish people had in their custody a valuable possession that set them above all of the civilizations before and after; they had possession of God's Words! They were given the priviledge of preserving and passing along the special revelation that God had given to His people in the Old Testament. More than any other people group, they were so close to the story of redemption that they missed out on making it personal. Paul goes on in Romans 9 to state that "I have great heaviness and continual sorrow in my heart." His heartache was generated by a genuine sadness over the general rejection of the Messiah. Instead of receiving Jesus as the Promised One, "He came unto his own, and his own received him not."

This truth is what is being illustrated by the older son in our parable. While the younger son ran away in his rebellion, the older son stayed at home in his rebellion. He had all the access to the father, his grace, and mercy; instead of embracing the goodness of the father, he rejects it and lives in his own world that is full of bitterness. It is possible to be near the father and yet be so far away.

SALVATION IN FOCUS #14 - Two Types of Sinners

When confronted with the goodness of the Savior, there are two responses of sinful hearts. The first type of response is typified by the younger son. He was living in sin and overwhelmed by the consequences of his separation from the father. Recognizing his own helplessness, he came to himself and made the turn toward home. That son was weak and dependent on the father's grace alone to restore him to fellowship. This is how some hearts respond; it is the heart cry of repentance from a soul that is trusting in Jesus alone to save!

The older son epitomizes the other type of response; some people are confronted with the gospel and yet refuse to submit to the goodness of the Savior. Instead of opening the heart to deal with the sin that is being exposed, they retreat to the safety of their own heart and pretend that things are well. Unrighteousness? No way! "I'm a good person. I was baptized when I was a child…my dad was a deacon in the church…I've been a member of the church for years." In essence, these are the words of the older son as he declared his own righteousness to the father and proudly pronounced he was to blame! That summarizes the two responses to the gospel: either humble submission or prideful rejection.

---

25 Now his elder son was in the field: and as he came and drew nigh to the house, he heard musick and dancing. 26 And he called one of the servants, and asked what these things meant.

It had been a long day in the fields. The older son wasn't a common laborer by any stretch of the imagination but the heat and sun had done its damage; he was ready for the coolness of the house. The elder son is introduced to the Pharisees in a manner that would immediately elevate their first impression of him - he was a hard worker! While the younger son was out squandering the family's wealth, the older son was doing what a noble son should be doing. He was supporting his father through faithful labor.

Hard work was an understatement in this first century Palestine culture. It was engrained into the culture because it was a fundamental aspect of the Old Testament law. As God had given each Jewish family a portion of the land, He expected them to make the land produce the food needed for their family to survive. The pattern of work was seen in Creation itself; God worked for the six days of creation and then rested on the seventh. Even those had lost access to land were still given the opportunity to participate in the harvest through the gleaning laws. No one was given a free ride. Everyone had to work; hard work made sense to the Pharisees.

Over the centuries, this mentality of hard work seeped into the religious system as well. While it was the early Christian Judaizers that actively taught that salvation was by works (Galatians 2), the Pharisees had constructed a system where obedience to the law and following traditions were the actions of the righteous and blessed. Those that did not fit into their system had no path to gain "God's favor" in their eyes; they placed heavier burdens on others to obey the ordinances of the Old Testament than they themselves were willing to observe.

The scribes and the Pharisees sit in Moses's seat: All therefore whatsoever they bid you observe, that observe and do; but do not ye after their works: for they say, and do not. For they bind heavy burdens and grievous to be borne, and lay them on men's shoulders; but they themselves will not move them with one of their fingers. Matthew 23:2-4

So as the older son comes near to the house he hears something that has been missing from his house for a long time: rejoicing! The music and dancing that hit his ears had been absent since his younger brother left with his inheritance. The illegitimate departure of his brother was devastating for his father and had created intense community tension. As he crested the hill and made the turn toward home, he was confused. "What does all this mean? Why is there rejoicing?" These are questions that he wanted answered! Getting the answers would be very simple; the older son just needed to go home and it all would be clear.

Though we have spent many chapters in this book uncovering the early parts of this parable, it is at this point where Jesus begins drawing the parable to a conclusion; the older son refuses to go home. Though at first it seems like he is just asking about the celebration, it becomes quickly clear that he has no desire to be a part of any party for his brother's return. He stops short of the house and calls out a servant. The Greek word that Jesus used in this verse implies a servant of young age (παῖς pais). It was a young servant child that became the intitial focus of his anger as he asked repeatedly about the celebration at the house. "Why is there a celebration? Why is there rejoicing?" You can almost sense in his reaction to the music and celebration that he is has already made up his mind to be angry, no matter what the celebration is about!

The young servant's answer was not what he wanted to hear. His younger brother had returned. This was a shock to his ears! "My brother is home? Is that the cause for celebration? Has my dad gone mad?" This was insane! His younger brother had absolutely destroyed his family and deserved nothing but shame and reproach! "I refuse to go home…I won't step one foot into that house with my scoundrel brother!"

Luke 15:28 And he was angry, and would not go in: therefore came his father out, and intreated him.

To a degree, his anger was understandable. His reaction is somewhat predictable. Like a father that can read the mind of his child, the father in our parable calmly comes out to talk to his older son. The Greek word that Jesus used for the father's intreating (παρακαλέω, parakaleo) means "to be near and comfort." While the father could have been angry at the son's reaction, he responded with the same grace that was offered to the younger son. The father's desire was clear…he wanted both sons to dwell together under one roof! As we read verses 29 and 30, it is clear that the older son had incredible confusion about what was happening all around him. Shortly, we will look at the older son's focus on his own good works; he was incredibly self-centered. First, however, we need to see the confusion that existed within the mind of the Jewish people.

I remember hearing a story once of two older ladies sitting on the front porch, enjoying the cool summer breeze. As the sun began to set on the horizon, the temperature dropped and the crickets began their chirping. Just then, the church next door started their evening choir practice. The melody rang out through the night and filled the air. One woman leaned over to the other and said, "My, they sure are singing beautifully tonight." The other woman responded, "I hear that they make their sounds by rubbing their legs together!" These two ladies were sitting on the same front porch, listening to the same sounds...and yet they were hearing two very different things. This conflict of messages about the identity of Jesus is best seen in the interaction that He had with His disciples in Matthew's Gospel.

When Jesus came into the coasts of Caesarea Philippi, he asked his disciples, saying, Whom do men say that I the Son of man am? 14 And they said, Some say that thou art John the Baptist: some, Elias; and others, Jeremias, or one of the prophets. 15 He saith unto them, But whom say ye that I am? 16 And Simon Peter answered and said, Thou art the Christ, the Son of the living God. Matthew 13:13-15

It was a simple question: "Who is Jesus?" It was a simple question with an answer that alluded many people. Now before you ridicule the unbelieving Jews of the day, remember that we have so much more of God's Revelation than they had at their time. We have the written record of the apostles, the history of the early church from the book of Acts, as well as John's Revelation of things to come. We have the full context while theirs was limited; yet there were still many that believed that Jesus was the Messiah! What we find is that the expectation of the people actually became a stumblingblock to their acknowledging that Jesus was the Christ. Many were looking for a Messiah that would fulfill the prophecy of Malachi 3:1 and come busting onto the scene. Some were hoping for a military leader that would lead an uprising against the oppressive Roman rule. Even the disciples were confused about Jesus's primary role as Messiah; we see them asking about the earthly kingdom right up to the point that Jesus ascended into heaven in Acts 1.

Not only was the older son confused with the loud and joyful celebration, he was also confused with the grace that the father was extending to his undeserving brother. It made no sense. The forgiveness made no sense. The mercy made no sense. His younger brother deserved nothing! Yet the father is giving him everything. It especially made no sense because he had been so faithful all those years and had never received any type of celebration!

29 And he answering said to his father, Lo, these many years do I serve thee, neither transgressed I at any time thy commandment: and yet thou never gavest me a kid, that I might make merry with my friends: 30 But as soon as this thy son was come, which hath devoured thy living with harlots, thou hast killed for him the fatted calf.

This is the ultimate demonstraton of pride, anger, and disrespect. Now we see the tables turn. At one point in this story the younger son was full of rebellion and pride; now we get to see the true colors of the older brother as well. As you read through these verses it becomes very clear that the elder brother wasn't angry at his younger brother...he was angry at the father! He was angered over the grace he had shown to the undeserving. He was angry that so many resources were being spent in celebration. He was angry that the father's best was being poored out on the repentant son!

There are four unique things we see in this interaction with the father that help us understand the mindset of the Pharisees of the day. First, the older son showed incredible disrespect to the father. Though the English word 'lo' seems rather unobtrusive, it carries a very heavy load grammatically. It comes from the word which is translated "behold." In essence, he was saying "Look, Dad!" Look at what I am getting ready to tell you. Look. I am sick and tired of being pushed aside for all I have done for you. It is at this point that we see the second indication of his rebellion. He compares his service to the father as slavery. "Lo, these may years do I serve thee." The word 'serve' comes from the Greek *doulos* which means "slave or slavery." He was comparing his work for the father as slavery. "Dad, I slaved away for you all these years, and you never did anything for me!" As a side note, if the time working for the father was so difficult, why didn't he just leave? He could have easily packed up his bags and hit the road; headed for a new town and fresh horizons. He didn't leave because he had too much to gain - he stood to inherit all that was left of the father's belongings.

That allows us to see the third clue to his rebellion; he was full of greed. He comes home to a celebration for his brother, and now he has to sit here and watch his dad squander away what he considered his inheritance; it was being wasted! In essence, he had the exact same attitude that younger son had at the very beginning of our story. "Dad, I don't care about you or your love...I only want what's coming to me!"

The fourth sign of the son's rebellion is seen through this statement, "Lo, these many years do I serve thee, neither transgressed I at any time thy commandment." Why did the older son think he was more worthy than his younger brother? Because he had obeyed all the rules! He had followed all of his dad's laws and had carried out his orders; he performed the duties of a son; he had stuck it out and toed the line for dear old pop. In his mind, that was what it took to earn the favor of the father. Yet, there was no connecting his service to the father to a relationship with him.

As this portion of our story comes to a close, we see a tragic and yet honest picture of the Pharisees of Jesus's day. They believed that God was only concerned about the external compliance to the law. They devised hundreds of trivial rules that pushed outward the limits of what God had given through Moses. They lifted them up as equal with God's Revelation and scorned those that did not meet up to their standard of righteousness. These rules, as well intentioned as they were, actually concealed the true purpose of God's law which was to point toward the coming Redeemer. Near and yet so far away. It is possible to be near to the father and yet never have a relationship with him.

SALVATION IN FOCUS #15 - Our Righteousness Doesn't Save

If there is anything that we can learn from the Pharisees, it is that obedience to the law is not what brings about salvation! They were zealous in their keeping of the law and in their obedience to the statutes of God's Word; yet in their obedience they missed out on the fact that all God demands is repentant faith. No matter how hard we try to live in a way that God would deem as a "good life", we are all failures! Even if you could keep the law it is powerless to save. No one is saved through obedience to the law in the same way that the older son wasn't any more righteous just because he 'slaved away' for his dad though he resented every minute of it. Praise the Lord... we are saved by faith!

Galatians 2:16 Knowing that a man is not justified by the works of the law, but by the faith of Jesus Christ, even we have believed in Jesus Christ, that we might be justified by the faith of Christ, and not by the works of the law: for by the works of the law shall no flesh be justified.

Chapter 13
Mercy Extended

Luke 15:31-32 And he said unto him, Son, thou art ever with me, and all that I have is thine. It was meet that we should make merry, and be glad: for this thy brother was dead, and is alive again; and was lost, and is found.

There are few things more distasteful than an ungrateful child. Imagine that we are strolling through the deli section of the local food mart. Our shopping trip is going well; we have found a few unexpected sales, and we are well on our way to hitting the checkout line. Then, out of blue, our shopping trip is interrupted by a sound so awful that it is feared by even the most seasoned shopper; it is the sound of an ungrateful child! Give me this...I want that! Please understand, we are not talking about a fussy child. My wife and I have four children that went with us to the store, sat in the cart, and had their fair share of meltdowns because it was naptime. Our kids also had times where their sinful nature was on open display, and they weren't ashamed to show it! The behavior that we are talking about is different; we bristle at the sound of a child that is unthankful for what has been provided and expects to get whatever he or she wants. It is far more repulsive to see a grown son act in the same way!

As we come to the end of the parable, we are confronted with something that goes against human nature; we naturally resist those that are full of pride and arrogance. The older son had just gotten something off his chest that he had been carrying for far too long; though it seemed harsh, he was convinced that his dad needed to hear everything he had said. Talk down to dad to show that he was nobodies child - check. Point out how that he had slaved away in the fields without recognition for years - check. Sharply point out that dad was wasting all the valuable resources that were rightfully his inheritance - check. It goes against human understanding that the father offered grace and mercy to his older son. His ungracious attitude is sickening; he deserved to be put in his place.

There are two times that grace is offered in this parable. First, the father offers undeserved favor to the younger son when he greets him with open arms. This is the most visible example of grace and is the one to which we are naturally drawn. The younger son accepts the good grace of the father and is restored to his position of sonship! We love this expression of grace! However, there is another demonstration of grace that is much less considered and not nearly as esteemed as the other; it is the father's grace that is fully extended to the older son. He was just as undeserving as his younger brother, though he was completely unaware of how withdrawn he was from the father.

"Son, thou art ever with me, and all that I have is thine." The father extends all the rights of sonship to the older brother; the son only has to follow the father back home. It seems so simple. The same offer of grace and mercy that brought the younger son back into fellowship with the father is freely offered to the rebellious older son as well! In the context of the passage, these are not empty words. The words of the father parallel the grace that God had extended to the followers of Jehovah for centuries. They had the same offer to come into fellowship with God, but it demanded that they be willing to come into the house...and come in God's way!

Sadly, in the same way that the older son's response is missing from the end of the story, there is a missing response from the staunch keepers of the law as well. John 1:10-11 states "He was in the world, and the world was made by him, and the world knew him not. He came unto his own, and his own received him not." For almost 1,500 years the Jewish people had full access to the prophecies of the Old Testament and God, through inspiration, revealed himself and illuminated the pathway to Jesus Christ, the coming Messiah. Yet with the pathway to redemption revealed and prophecies being fulfilled before their own eyes, the majority of the Jewish religous leaders were blind to the presence of the Messiah. It is a thrill to report that there were some that did trust in Christ!

How do we know that grace was equally offered to the Pharisees? Because there were at least three Pharisees that we know accepted that grace and were restored to sonship! Consider briefly these men from the Scriptures. First, we see a man named Nicodemus from John 3. He was a high ranking ruler within the Jewish community and was seeking Truth from the one that came to give Truth. He approached Jesus one evening under the cover of darkness. The pressures from the other Jewish unbelievers was so intense that his only opportunity to speak to The Master was in the dimness of the night. Not only did Nicodemus come to Jesus, he came asking all the right questions! He spoke of Christ's deity. He affirmed His identity. There were questions about being born again and being born of the Spirit. Nicodemus reveals to us that his heart was searching; he had come to the right place to find the answers!

Jesus's response to Nicodemus was kind and compassionate. He walked Nicodemus through the gospel in the same way that he cared for the spiritual needs of His disciples. There was no harshness in Christ's voice - only an extension of grace and mercy to one that had once opposed Him. Nicodemus's response? Well, the Scriptures remain fairly quiet about Nicodemus and his response. In fact, it seems as though he walks away confused having rejected the offer of salvation that was extended. John 3, however, isn't the end of the story for Nicodemus! As we move through the book of John we come to our Savior hanging on the cross in chapter nineteen. His lifeless body remained hanging on the cross; onlookers were unsure if they were allowed to bring His body down. John 19:39-40 states, "And there came also Nicodemus, which at the first came to Jesus by night, and brought a mixture of myrrh and aloes, about an hundred pound weight. Then took they the body of Jesus, and wound it in linen clothes with the spices, as the manner of the Jews is to bury." Now Nicodemus wasn't alone; we will discuss the other man shortly. However, in that moment, Nicodemus did something that Peter, James, Matthew, Simon, and Thomas didn't do; he took care of the lifeless body of the Savior. While John doesn't reference Nicodemus directly as a disciple, his actions at the cross speak to his changed heart toward The Master that had offered him eternal life.

Nicodemus wasn't the only one to help take Jesus off the cross. Joseph of Arimathaea was also present and helped remove Jesus that day. While the Scriptures contain less information about this man than even Nicodemus, what we are told is very insightful and reveals his spiritual condition. First, we are told that he was part of the Sanhedrin - the group of men that called for the crucifixion. Luke's gospel account reveals that Joseph stood in opposition to that decision (Luke 23:51). Why? Because secretly he was a follower of the Messiah! Mark describes him as a man that was waiting for the kingdom of God. John refers to him as a secret disciple of Jesus; he was fearful of what the Pharisees would do to him if he confessed Jesus. Though he didn't openly follow Jesus as he walked the shores of Galilee or sit under his teaching as he told his disciples of things to come, Joseph was one of the Pharisees that heard the gracious call of the Savior and responded!

The third Pharisee conversion that we learn about in Scripture is someone that is slightly more well known - the Apostle Paul! While we know Paul as a great statesman for the faith through reading Acts and we learn from his letters to the early churches, Paul started his journey as a devout Jewish boy that learned the law under the best teachers. Paul's self description in Philippians 3 is eye opening; he was the older son in our story in every way!

Circumcised the eighth day, of the stock of Israel, of the tribe of Benjamin, an Hebrew of the Hebrews; as touching the law, a Pharisee; Concerning zeal, persecuting the church; touching the righteousness which is in the law, blameless. Philippians 3:5-6

His religous pride drove him to oppose the father's mercy in ways that are difficult to imagine. Paul (then Saul) was The Great Persecutor of the early church; he prided himself in detecting believers and rooting them out to be imprisoned. Scripture records that he "breathed out threatenings and slaughter" against those that followed the teachings of Jesus. In fact, Paul (of his own bidding) sought permission to go to

Damascus to uncover a group of believers and send them to prison. Paul actively opposed the mercy and grace of Jesus; all of this while considering himself a keeper of the law.

Just like the older son, Paul was close to the father and yet so far away from him.

This all changed with a flash of light. It was on the road to Damascus that God graciously extended His mercy to Paul; this parallels the father coming out to speak to his older son in our parable. Confronted by the very one that had been the focus of his persecution, Paul humbled himself before the Lord! In a response not seen by the older son in our parable, Paul did not refuse the offer of grace from the Father but rather embraced Him and chose to be a part of the celebration. Paul was no longer "far away"; through salvation he was brought back into fellowship with the Father!

SALVATION IN FOCUS #16 - God's Gracious Call

Is the offer of salvation for everyone or only for a select group of people? Does God unconditionally choose who will come to Him in faith? Was the offer of mercy to the older son a genuine call to repentance? These are core questions that drive us deep into the Scriptures and are somewhat defining in our conversation about salvation. From Christ's teaching on salvation, let's consider the pattern He gives in regards to these issues.

1. Is the offer of salvation for everyone or only for a select group? The father's interaction with his two sons clearly demonstrates that salvation is available to everyone; to those that respond (younger son) as well as those that reject (older son).

2. Does God unconditionally chose who will come to him in faith? What Jesus illustrates in this parable is a grace that is open to all that will repent, regardless of their past sins or religious connections. Either the father's gentle pleading for the older son's restoration was genuine, or it was manufactured and artificial.

3. Is the call of the father irresistable? What we see in this passage is quite the opposite. The younger son, with knowledge of his own helplessness and the father's ability to save, humbly responds to that 'good news' and makes the repentant turn toward the father. The older son, hardened by his years of ungratefulness and pride, refuses the father's gracious call to come to the house and join in the celebration.

...And then there were crickets.

What was the older son's response? Did he choose to join in the celebration? This parable has such an abrupt ending that it leaves the reader hanging. There is no clear resolution to the situation that we have been presented; the father and older son are standing in the field, looking at the house, standing in silence. Suspense is an incredible literary tool that good writers weave into their story to keep the reader holding on till the very end. However, a good suspense writer knows how to finish the story! There is nothing more satisfying than coming to the end of a gripping mystery novel and seeing the pieces to the story fit together as you come to the final page. We are at that point in our story! Except, instead of using the tool of suspense and resolution, Jesus uses suspense and uncertainty. He doesn't resolve the tension at the end of the parable. It just ends.

This is an incredible tactic that Jesus used quite effectively in this story. Its effectiveness is built on the fact that the story has a defined structure that is predictable when you step back and consider how the story progresses. Let's reflect first on the younger son's half of the story and its progression.

    A - the son is dead to the father
        B - the son loses all of the inheritance
            C - the son is alone and cast aside
                D - the son is hungry and in desperate need
                D - the son recognizes that his father has plenty
            C - the son is embraced by the father
        B - the son is restored to his position of son
    A - the son was dead and now is alive

There is hidden beauty in the parallelism of the Parable of

the Prodigal Son that we don't even see when we read through it so quickly; it is only seen when we step back and look at the beauty of the poetic structure. Jesus spoke in a way that took the listener on a journey of emotions that began with the cultural death of the son and ended at the joyous reunion with the father. Jesus presents the story this way for two reasons. First, it is an effective manner of building emotion within a narrative. Tragedy, loss, need, realization, turning, cry for help, restoration, rejoicing: You could write almost any story using this pattern and be able to connect the reader to the characters and as a result communicate intense emotion. The second reason that Jesus used this pattern is simple. He was setting the listeners up for an unresolved ending. That's right; the parable actually lacks a formal ending! As we come to the final plea from the father the parable ends so abruptly that you can almost miss the fact that you have moved on. However, the lack of resolution created a tension within the story that left the Pharisees stunned and speechless. Consider the progression of the second half of Christ's parable and you will see the unresolved ending was not an accident.[21]

---

[21] Kenneth Bailey, Finding the Lost Cultural Keys to Luke 15 (St. Louis, Concordia Press, 1992), 148.

   A - older son stands away in the field
      B - older son is angry over his brother
         C - the father's gracious approach
            D - older son focuses on his right actions
            D - older son focuses on his brother's actions
         C - the father's gracious appeal
      B - the father's joy over the return of the younger son
A - NOTHING!

That's it. The parable ends without ever knowing what action the older brother in the story took. Did he join the celebration? Was there a family reunion with the entire family? Those are questions that Jesus left unanswered on purpose. You see, the ball was now in the Pharisees' court. Their response to the gospel was dependent on their response to the gracious call to join the celebration. We know that there were some that did respond; we looked at their testimonies earlier in this chapter. However, the vast majority of the Pharisees remained in their unbelief, blinded by their own religous tradition. It is possible to be close to the father and yet to be far from him in your heart.

Though the parable ends rather abruptly in Luke 15, I am here to tell you that the ending of the parable is actually contained in Scripture! That's right — a hidden ending that is so often overlooked that you might be surprised to hear that it even exists. Any guesses where it is found? To fully understand how the parable ended, consider that the parable (as it was given) only had two possible endings. It either ended with the older brother reconciling to the father and joining in the celebration, or it ended with him remaining outside and distant from the father's grace. Here is how those two may have played out. Please understand that these are not quotes from Scripture but were simply written to replicate the two options.

Luke 15:31-32 31 "And he said unto him, Son, thou art ever with me, and all that I have is thine. 32 It was meet that we should make merry, and be glad: for this thy brother was dead, and is alive again; and was lost, and is found..."

Possible Option #1

...Then the elder son, seeing the love of his father and being moved by his tender mercies, fell on his knees and said, "Father, I repent for my bitter spirit, for my heart of anger toward your kindness. I too am not worthy to be called your son. Father, please forgive me for my rebellious spirit." Then the father, moved with compassion, fell on the older son's neck and cried great tears of joy, and took the older son by the hand and they joined together in the celebration of the father's mercy and grace. Thus they celebrated that both sons were lost, but now had been found. Both were dead, and yet now were made alive again!

Possible Option #2

...Then the elder son, being full of anger over his father's love for the younger son, became bitter and hardened to the love of the father. From that day forward he refused to rejoice over his younger brother's return — the lingering anger was more than his heart could control. Prompted by the prolonged resentment, the older son was moved to action. Luring the gracious father into the garden, the older son lashed out in fury and struck his father so that he died.

As harsh as Option #2 seems...that is exactly what happened. All through Christ's earthly ministry He preached grace and mercy to all that would respond. This is evidenced by the number of people that came to faith under his preaching. The call to repent was given, and the listeners were presented with the choice to believe and receive or reject the gospel message. Coincidentally, many of the Jewish leaders followed in the exact path that the older son had set himself toward. There was a pride in their heart and a refusal to accept the gracious call of the Savior. This pride kept them outside the fathers house; they refused to come in to the celebration of the father's grace and mercy.

This refusal of the Savior was more than just a surface rejection — they desired to see him killed. Often in the New Testament we hear of the Pharisees' anger over the words of Jesus. This anger was deep. The hatred that they had for Jesus drove them to plot his death and eventually deliver Him up to the Romans to be tried and punished. Even after the Roman authorities cleared Him of all charges, the persistent cries to crucify Jesus demonstrated that it wasn't about guilt or innocence — it was about rejection. They rejected Him as the Messiah. They rejected his offer of grace and mercy. They refused to come into the 'house' and be brought back into fellowship with their Messiah. They led Jesus outside of the city, and after mocking and reviling our Saviour, they crucified Him on a cross made of rough wooden timbers. Their hatred for Jesus Christ and rejection of his free offer of salvation culminated in His death. This is the true ending of the parable.

Modern Day Pharisees

In the same way that the Pharisees in Christ's day struggled with their righteousness coming from something other than rules and traditions, we can stumble along the same path in our endeavor to live righteously before God. In fact, it is easy to slip into the same trappings of rules and traditions they struggled with; we can easily depend on our position in relation to others to become the indicator of our spirituality. Consider these eight indicators that the spirit of the older brother has crept into your spiritual walk.

1. Church activity equals spirituality.

The older son was very proud of all the years that he had 'slaved' away for the father. It was his service to the father that made him more deserving and praiseworthy. When our actions become the basis for our worth to God, we have become just like the Pharisees.

2. Rules become the focus.

Pharisees love to argue. There is always something that they are against, someone that they are opposing, or some new behavior that must be avoided. In fact, Pharisees have a hard time separating all the things they are against from the gospel message. To a great extent, the Pharisees of Jesus's day were more concerned with obeying their set of rules than following in the footsteps of the Savior.

3. You think God needs you.

Do you remember the words of the older son? He was confident that his service to the father was deserving of praise and recognition. He was angered that his efforts were unappreciated.

4. Bible study is to prove what you believe.

No one knew the Scriptures better than the Scribes and Pharisees of Jesus's day. However, they failed to use their knowledge in a way that actually drew them to an understanding of the Messiah. Instead, their grasp of the Old Testament accomplished little more than substantiating their works based religion.

5. You must conform to a standard.

Because the Christian life is about a set of rules, conformity to those rules becomes the yardstick by which your spirituality is judged. In fact, some will go so far as to deny the loving grace of the father (through preaching, church attendance, fellowship) unless there is conformity to the established standards.

6. Pharisees are easily angered when confronted.

The father extended a gracious plea to the older son, and his response was full of anger and bitterness. Pharisees can't afford to be confronted over their distance from the father. When this happens, they go into full attack mode.

7. Your sin isn't that bad.

The younger son deserved to be disowned; he was a disgrace to the family. The older son, however, didn't need to repent of his anger or bitterness. The sins of the Pharisees are never that bad compared to the sins of others.

8. You are angered when God offers grace to the unlovely.

When sinners are brought to repentance, is your heart filled with joy? When the enemies of God are granted grace and mercy, a hesitant joy indicates the presence of a Pharisaical spirit. God has the right to grant grace and mercy to whomever He wills! We should rejoice when our enemies are spared and are able to taste the goodness of the Lord!

When the older son was confronted by his distance from the father, he responded with excuses, anger, and finger-pointing. His actions become a pattern by which we can (and should) judge our own standing with the Father. The reality is that the Pharisees were content to remain distant from Jesus and continue their existence in the "fields" of religion and tradition. Just as the father extended grace to the older son, the gracious sacrifice of Jesus Christ is sufficent to save even the worst sinner!

Your Story

What about the end of your story? The gracious offer of redemption is just as available to you today as it was to the Pharisees in Jesus's day. What will you do with Jesus? Which son best represents your response to the gracious father? One possiblity is that you will sit apart from Jesus's grace and mercy, filled with pride and held back by your own self-worth. The other option? The heart cry of repentance! "Dear Jesus, I know that my sins have separated me from your goodness. Jesus, my sins are wicked in your sight, and I am not worthy to be called your son. Jesus, I believe that it is only through your grace and mercy that I can be forgiven. I believe that you died for me and bore my shame, and I am depending only on your strength to restore my soul. Humbly, I come to you, acknowledging that only you are powerful to save!" It is only when we come to Christ in humble faith that we can truly see salvation through the eyes of the prodigal son!

Epilogue
Common Misconceptions

I will be honest with you...this is not a chapter that I planned on writing when I set out to compose this book. My desire was to bring the parable to an end and then to allow the truths from the passage to settle in and do their work. Sometimes the words "The End" are very elusive. Often our best laid plans take detours that we did not intend; from time to time we are forced to accept that there is more work to be done, and the job is not complete. Over the several months of this writing, I have had several insightful discussions with friends in the ministry that have revealed that this book needs this final chapter. Though we have come to several conclusions from the words of Jesus in Luke 15, not everyone comes to those same conclusions. To be frank, not everyone is 'free' to allow the text to speak so plainly about man's sin, repentance, forgiveness, and restoration. For some, doing so would go against the very foundations of their soteriology.

It was through conversations with friends and aquaintances that I became aware of such a pushback against what I feel is the obvious and intended interpretation of Luke 15. I was introduced to several arguments as to why this interpretation is invalid; it became obvious that these objections, while easily dismissed, can create significant doubt if not thought through in a careful manner. In fact, it was with you (the reader) in mind that I decided to write this chapter and address a few of the more 'convincing' objections. My desire is that you will be able to take the illustration of salvation that Jesus Christ lays out for us in Luke 15 and use it to accurately communicate the gospel. Inevitably, doing so would invite the skepticism of critics and force you to defend your point of interpretation. After having studied the passage in depth and seeing Christ's clear and obvious purpose, I am confident that you could articulate many of these on your own. However, in the next few pages I would like to present to you many of the common arguments against our interpretation in the hopes that they would strengthen your understanding of Christ's wonderful words of salvation in the Parable of the Prodigal Son.

Objection #1 - The Parable of the Prodigal Son isn't about salvation.

This is covered first for two reasons. First, it goes to the very heart of our interpretation. If the context of Luke 15 isn't salvation, then we have to throw out everything that pertains to salvation that we have covered in all of the previous chapters. Think of how much of this book would be considered "in error" if the context of this passage has nothing to do with salvation. The second reason why we cover this objection first is that it is likely the first objection that you will hear when talking to those that take exception to this interpretation. It is simply the "low hanging fruit" that most often gets thrown first.

Let's look at it from their perspective first. If the parable isn't about salvation then what is it about? The answers may vary slightly, but they inevitably come to this conclusion; the parable is about (1) God's grace poured out on those that rebel against him and (2) the shameful behavior of the Pharisees in not rejoicing over that grace. This position makes a very subtle and yet fundamental assumption that the younger son represents a backslidden believer. While we freely acknowledge that the Pharisees' response to Jesus's gracious interactions with the undeserving is at the center of the overall purpose of the chapter, you have to establish the identity of the recipients of that grace. Whoever was receiving the grace in Luke 15:1-2 is at the same time identified as the lost coin, the lost sheep, and the lost/dead son. In other words, were the Pharisees upset that Jesus fellowshipped with backslidden Christians or with sinners? That simple question lies at the heart of this objection.

While it is Luke that records his gospel account, it is the words of Jesus Christ Himself that declare the identity of those recipients. They were sinners! The Pharisees were upset that Jesus was eating and offering undeserved favor on sinners. Were they just 'backslidden Christians' that were overwhelmed with their sin? Absolutely not. That is why twice in this chapter Jesus declares that there is rejoicing in heaven over one sinner that comes to repentance. The joy is over the finding of the lost coin, the lost sheep, the lost son...a lost soul!

Why is this important? If we concede that the parable is about God's grace on rebellious believers, we must somehow undo the cultural implications of the younger son's rebellion. There could be no real guilt for the younger son's actions, for "there is therefore now no condemnation to them which are in Christ Jesus." (Romans 8:1) The younger son's wasting of his inheritance must be viewed as a believer's squandering all that we have as heirs of God and joint heirs with Christ. (Romans 8:17) There would have been no need for the younger son's 'come to himself' moment; he could have walked confidently back home and expected all the rights of sonship because he was still a son!

If for no other reason, there is a consistency in interpretation that demands that the Parable of the Prodigal Son center around the salvation of the lost. When we consider the interpretation of a passage, it is imperative to take the cultural, Scriptural, and circumstantial context in mind. None of these have changed within Luke 15. The words in the first ten verses are spoken to the same people under the same circumstances with an identical purpose as the last twenty-two verses. To insert an arbitrary division within the chapter that changes the interpretation is dangerous as a student of the Scriptures and can easily result in interpretations that are not true to the text. If it is clear through Christ's own words that the first two parables focus on the rejoicing in heaven over sinners that come to repentance, then we should take great care not to alter that clear directive as we interpret the final of the three parables.

One last thought. Never in Scripture are believers ever referred to as 'lost' or 'dead.' Those are terms reserved for those that have never come to faith and are still "dead in their trespasses and sins." It would be totally inconsistent within the passage for the younger son to represent a rebellious believer and yet the lost coin and lost sheep clearly represent a lost soul that comes to repentance. Those are Christ's very words! Identifying the younger son as a rebellious believer makes no sense within the passage and forces the interpretation well beyond the normal and plain meaning of the parable as Jesus gave it to the listeners.

Objection #2 - The younger son was always a son.

If the first objection demonstrates a lack of discernment surrounding the context of the passage, this one reveals a lack of consideration of the cultural context. This objection is often framed through this type of argument: "At the beginning of the story the younger son was a son. In the middle he was a son. At the end he was still a son. Though he walked away from the father, he was still a son. It would be wrong to consider him 'lost' or a 'sinner' while feeding the swine within the parable; unless you believe that a person can be saved (a son) and then lose his salvation, you must always consider the younger son as part of God's family."

There are two points where this objection falls apart; the first is on the grounds of cultural context. To say that the son in the parable was always a son is culturally incorrect. I realize that in Western cultures there is a connection that children have to their parents no matter what they do to shame the family. I have heard personal accounts from local maximum security prison guards as they tell of the overwhelming number of parents and family members that come out for "family day" at the prison. Sons that have committed wicked and shameful things are embraced and celebrated by parents and spouses. Though they are guilty of the worst that society can imagine, the prison is inundated with family members who want to see their loved one.

Jesus Christ was not speaking to our Westernized culture. Behavior that brings shame to family is dealt with harshly; a rebellious son is not embraced as a son but is shunned and disowned by the family and community. This honor/shame dyamic still exists today in many parts of the world and is the driving force within many cultures. In fact, the phrase "you are dead to me" has two very real connections within the parable. Think back to the demand that the younger son made to his father. "Dad, though you aren't dead yet, you are dead to me...I want my inheritance and I am leaving!" The son's unimaginable demand communicated clearly to his father that he wanted out of the family! On the other side, do you remember the words that Jesus gave to the father as he embraced his wayward son back home? "For this my son was dead, and is alive again; he was lost, and is found." The father clearly verbalizes the son's deadness to the family...he had been disowned by the culture. To view the family dynamic in this passage only through Western eyes completely misses the reality that Jesus was speaking to people that lived in a completely different culture.

The second way in which this objection looses ground is often seen in the followup response to what we just established. "Are you saying that a person can be a son (saved) and then choose to walk away and lose his salvation, only to return and be welcomed back into God's family?" The answer is a simple "No." To make this claim or bring up this objection fails to recognize that we don't have to rebel to be put out of God's family, we are all born that way! Romans 5:12 states clearly that "...as by one man sin entered into the world, and death by sin; and so death passed upon all men, for that all have sinned." Adam was the only man born into fellowship with God. In the same way that the younger son squandered the inheritance of the father, Adam turned his back on the Father and squandered away all the blessings and goodness that God had given to mankind in the perfect world. In seeking to be as a god (Genesis 3:5), Adam turned his back on the Heavenly Father; Adam was forced out the garden. He was spiritually disowned and cast aside. He was no longer a 'child of God' by nature.

It is in this state of spiritual separation that we are all born. I didn't have to rebel against my heavenly Father, I was born in rebellion. You were too! In a spiritual sense, you were born separated from the Father, feeding the swine, with no hope of saving yourself. You see, no one has to lose their salvation in order to become the 'prodigal son.' We are wayward and apart from God from our very entrance into the world! So while the younger son in the parable was still the progeny of the father, in reality he was dead to the father and no longer part of the family. With that in mind, the younger son's position and relationship with the father illustrate a lost soul perfectly...just as Jesus intended!

Objection #3 - God is the father, not Jesus.

While this is not the most obvious objection, it is one that I have heard nonetheless. If you can argue against the identity of the younger son, you can also argue against the identity of the father in the parable. Who is the father? Well, the easiest conclusion would be that the father represents God the Father. Why? Because they both have the name 'father.' It seems simple enough! Sadly, that is as deep as some would like to go in their pursuit of Christ's teaching in this chapter. Thankfully we have laid enough of a foundation that the identity of the father should be relatively easy to uncover.

The entire chapter was written to demonstrate the attitude of the Pharisees toward Jesus's gracious encounter with sinners in their community. So there were three groups that needed to be addressed in the parable. First were the sinners — the youngest son. Then there were the Pharisees — the older son. That leaves only Jesus! It is completely fitting soteriologically that Jesus is at the center of this story of redemption...He is the epicenter of the entire story of redemption! Jesus Christ was at the center of creation. Jesus Christ was the focus of propecy. Jesus was central to the plan of redemption. Jesus's life is the hinge on which history turns. Jesus's earthly experience was the central focus of God's love toward mankind.

Objection #4 - There is no mention of Christ's sacrifice in the parable.

Usually this objection is framed in this manner — "The father can't represent Jesus Christ and His offer of salvation since there is no mention of Christ's atoning sacrifice in the parable." This is an objection that is impossible to disprove. In fact, it is completely accurate to say that there is no mention of Christ's atoning sacrifice within the parable. However, does the absence of that detail necessarily mean that you must recontextualize the entire chapter? No! In fact, this objection is nothing more than two separate logical fallacies crammed into one objection.

First, this argument commits the logical fallacy called "moving the goalposts." This occurs when the standard for the discussion is moved higher and higher within the conversation...often moving it beyond what is possible to establish. No one would ever start with this objection, but often this becomes a second or third attempt to derail a salvific interpretation of the parable. In essence, it is setting up the absence of evidence within the parable as evidence for their position. This leads us to the second logical fallacy called "argument from silence." This fallacy of logic assumes that if the one argument they are making (Christ's sacrifice) is missing from the parable, then it is established that the parable cannot be about salvation. Do you see how the goalposts have been raised? Instead of allowing the words that Jesus gave speak for themselves, the standard is being raised above the text.

While this objection is a simple logical fallacy, the consequences of this argument are serious — the focus of the attack is Jesus Christ Himself. It assumes that we know better than Jesus what elements need to be included in order make the parable effective. As Jesus spoke these words He gave everything that was necessary and needed to make His point clear and complete to the listeners. He included everything that needed to be included and left out everything that need to be left out. To argue otherwise is to accuse Jesus of being incomplete in the details of the parable.

Objection #5 - It is wrong to teach doctrine from a parable.

Well, sort of. While this objection seems to be an attempt to protect the Scriptures — to keep it from being twisted and contorted — it actually makes an assumption that is false. It is false to say that a parable cannot teach doctrine. If a parable was given within the context of doctrine then it would be completely appropriate to let that parable speak to which it was given. Parables about the kingdom teach us truths about the gospel, how it is received, and how it is spread. Parables about eschatology teach us truths about Christ's coming, the end times, and the eternal fate of the lost. In that sense, parables that were given in the context of a lost soul coming to repentance (Jesus's own words in Luke 15) can and should be interpreted completely within the context of that doctrine.

There is a form of this objection that is completely valid, though it does not really apply in our situation. It would state that it is wrong to "form" or "base" a doctrine from a parable. That would be completely accurate! Yes! It would be completely inappropriate and theologically foolish to use parables as the foundation for our doctrine. Parables were never meant to establish doctrine but were cast alongside a theological truth in order to make that truth more understandable. It would be very dangerous to take a parable, no matter how complex and intricate, and form your doctrine around that genre of teaching. Parables simply do not teach doctrine.

To be clear, we have not used the Parable of the Prodigal son that way in this book. While we have looked at the doctrine of salvation and clearly tried to understand all the contextual clues that Jesus Christ used, the Parable of the Prodigal Son is thrown alongside passages like John 3 and Romans 1-8. Those are the texts that establish our understanding of salvation. Luke

15 just helps illustrate the doctrine that Scripture clearly establishes elsewhere.

Objection #6 - When interpreting a parable, there is one and only one point.

This final objection is based on the desire to protect the extent to which a parable is interpreted. In other words, let's not take parables too far...let's not make parables say things they weren't intended to say. This argument stems from a true understanding of parables — they were given to teach or reveal a specific truth rather than teach broad truths. What we have to establish with this parable is the extent to which that one truth is revealed within the text. In other words, we must establish how far you can take the Parable of the Prodigal Son and still be within the bounds of proper interpretation.

The 'one truth' of this parable is simple — the Pharisees refused to rejoice over the offer of grace to undeserving sinners. In its simplicity, however, we just introduced the doctrine of salvation! To put it another way, it is impossible to remove the illustration of salvation from the parable because it is within this illustration that the hard hearted Pharisees are revealed. When this objection is raised, it is usually on the basis of excluding salvation from the picture all together. The context simply won't allow us to do that! If we remove any mention of salvation or refuse to recognize that the younger son illustrates mankind that is lost and dead in sin, then what are the

Pharisees upset about? Seriously! We have removed the very thing that Jesus intended to illustrate in the first place! While we would agree that it is dangerous to take a parable's interpretation too far, it is clear that the salvation of the lost is right in line with the proper explanation of this parable.

The End

Recommended Resources

Throughout the writing of this book I have referenced many printed works that have helped me along the way. Though not all of them have been cited directly within this book, they were all helpful in gaining a better understanding of the culture and context that Christ's Parable of the Prodigal Son was given. This brief list includes the books that were extremely helpful in my study. Please refer to the book's footnotes for specific citations within this book.

Bailey, Kenneth E. *Finding the Lost Cultural Keys to Luke 15*. St Louis: Concordia House Publishing, 1992.

Bailey, Kenneth E. *Jesus Through Middle Eastern Eyes: Cultural Studies in the Gospels*. Downers Grove, IL: IVP Academic, 2009.

Georges, Jayson. *The 3D Gospel: Ministry in Guilt, Shame, and Fear Cultures*. US: Time Press, 2017.

Hartman, Craig. *Through Jewish Eyes*. Greenville, SC: BJU Press, 2010.

Hunt, David and James White. *Debating Calvinism*. Sisters, OR: Multnomah Press, 2004.

Jeremias, Joachim. *The Parables of Jesus*. London: SCM Press LTD, 1954.

Laniak, Timothy S. *Shame and Honor in the Book of Esther*. Atlanta: Society of Biblical Liturature, 1998.

Lees, G. Robinson. *Village Life in Palestine*. London: Longman, Greene and Company, 1905.

MacArthur, John. *A Tale of Two Sons*. Nashville: Thomas Nelson Publishing, 2008.

Pentecost, J. Dwight. *The Parables of Jesus*. Grand Rapids, MI: Kregal Publishing, 1982.

Connect With The Author!

I want to invite you to connect with me! Here are three ways you can make it happen.

1. Visit www.djharry.org/connect and join my early readers group. Whenever a new book is published I always give away free digital copies and will select some on that list to receive a free advanced reader copy as well. I value your insight and would love for you to join my team!

2. Suscribe to Let's Talk Church and become a listener! The discussion centers around ministry issues and is helpful for anyone that is involved in local church ministry. Visit www.letstalk.church for more information.

3. Connect with me on social media! I love to connect online with listeners and readers and would love for us to connect there as well. Search for @PastorDJHarry on Facebook and Twitter and Pastor.DJHarry on Instagram.

Pastor DJ Harry

Made in the USA
Columbia, SC
06 September 2018